STORIES OF HOPE

STORIES OF HOPE

Living in Serenity with Chronic Pain and Chronic Illness

CHRONIC PAIN ANONYMOUS SERVICE BOARD

ISBN: 978-0-9856524-0-1

Library of Congress Control Number: 2012944013

Chronic Pain Anonymous Service Board
8912 E. Pinnacle Peak Road
Suite F9-628
Scottsdale AZ 85255

Email: *literature@chronicpainanonymous.org*

Website: *chronicpainanonymous.org*

Approved by Chronic Pain Anonymous Service Board

First Edition

By following the Steps of Chronic Pain Anonymous, my relationship with chronic pain and chronic illness is no longer adversarial. Each morning I wake with the joy of hope. Challenges no longer block the way. Possibilities I never dreamed of are now part of my daily existence.

Dale L. – Baltimore, MD
Co-founder of CPA

CPA Serenity Prayer

God, grant me the serenity
to accept the things I cannot change,
The courage to change the
things I can,
and the wisdom to
know the difference.
Thy will, not mine, be done.

CONTENTS

Preface xi

Introduction xiii

Pain 1

Loss 9

Fear and Anger 12

Acceptance 19

Trust 32

Faith 38

Surrender 50

Courage 60

Accountability 65

Strength 79

Attitude 86

Fellowship 99

Freedom from the Bondage of Self 108

One Day at a Time 113

Self-Care 116

Joy 131

Hope 137

Appendices

The Twelve Steps of Chronic Pain Anonymous 145

The Twelve Traditions of Chronic Pain Anonymous 146

One Day at a Time 147

Index 149

Literature available from Chronic Pain Anonymous 155

Notes 156

PREFACE

Dale L. and Barry M. co-founded Chronic Pain Anonymous (CPA) in 2004 in order to apply the Steps, concepts and tools of Alcoholics Anonymous to living with chronic pain and chronic illness. Recovery in CPA is defined as the ability to live peacefully, joyfully, and happily with oneself and others. The Twelve Steps and Twelve Traditions are the essence of the CPA program, helping to create a life of serenity, regardless of physical circumstances.

CPA is a fellowship of men and women who share their experience, strength and hope with each other so that they may solve their common problem and help others recover from the disabling effects of chronic pain and chronic illness. The only requirement for membership is a desire to recover from the emotional and spiritual debilitation of chronic pain or chronic illness. There are no dues or fees for CPA membership. We are self-supporting through our own contributions. CPA does not ally with any organization or institution.

Our primary purpose is to live our lives to the fullest by minimizing the effects of chronic pain and chronic illness in our lives and helping others to do the same. We do this by practicing the Twelve Steps and welcoming and giving comfort and understanding to each other.

INTRODUCTION
Stories of Hope

Twelve Step programs are designed for those of us with an obsession that controls our life and interferes with our peace of mind. Whether it is alcohol, narcotics, or food, the guidance of these recovery programs creates a new way to relate to the object of intense focus. As a result, we are able to navigate each day with ease and inner confidence. The successful tools that form the foundation of all Twelve Step programs are based on spiritual principles. The members of Chronic Pain Anonymous (CPA) discovered that these same tools provide a solution to the emotional and mental anguish that derives from chronic pain and chronic illness.

By using the Twelve Steps, CPA members experience contentment and harmony, and a life once again filled with hope for new possibilities. The Steps guide us back to a life we love, taking us on a spiritual journey in which we develop a personal relationship with a Power greater than ourselves. We examine the part we play in our own suffering, heal past wounds, and awaken forgiveness, compassion and acceptance. Three main tools of the program—meetings, the Twelve Steps, and service—support us in the process.

Many of us take a long, exhausting, sometimes expensive road—through visits to family doctors, medical specialists, and alternative care practitioners, possibly invasive procedures and even metaphysical studies—searching for cures. We desperately seek to control and eliminate the problem we believe keeps us from being who we once were and who we want to be today. We try everything . . . often losing much along the way. Our lives are taken over by our attempts to find relief, and yet we are still filled with despair and defeat. Fear keeps us clinging to the past and dreading the future, while negative stories and expectations add to our stress. For many of us there is nothing more to try, and we are ready to give up.

Feeling misunderstood by our friends, family, or the medical community, we worry that we are now defined by our illness and pain, cut off from past relationships and life accomplishments. Due to our condition, we become isolated, accompanied by fear, shame, grief, and anger. We feel lost and helpless.

CPA is about a different way to live. The Twelve Step-inspired journey of discovery leads us to recognize that while we may not be able to heal our bodies, we can heal our minds and spirits. We develop a new relationship to our pain and illness. In *Stories of Hope* you will learn how others came to be at peace with their circumstances, expanding their bodies and minds to include joy. The thread of hope is woven throughout these pages, written by men and women who have been freed of the mental, emotional, and spiritual obstacles that have kept them from full participation in the world. Life may be *different* than what they had imagined previously, yet as you will see it is rewarding and fulfilling in unexpected and refreshing ways.

These anonymous words tell our stories. Reading them, we realize we are no longer alone. These are people who live like us, with chronic pain and chronic illness, people who once thought all hope was lost, but have uncovered hidden strength and courage. Their stories demonstrate how well-being *can* be ours. They found self-compassion, dignity and acceptance, and so can we. Hope is sparked in knowing that the past does not determine our future.

Stories of Hope is divided into topics, leading the reader from pain, loss, fear and anger, to changed attitudes and new patterns of behavior that make possible a different way of life. In these pages you will learn how to shift your perspective, by being willing to commit to new ways of thinking and acting, and becoming teachable. You will begin to understand that chronic pain and chronic illness do not mean the end of life, just a new chapter. Happiness and serenity *are* compatible with physical pain and disease.

Growing in acceptance, we learn to live in the reality of the present, letting go of our attachment to how we think things should be. As we learn new skills, we naturally eliminate negative behaviors. Widening our focus beyond our self-centered needs, we shift from insecurity and fear to humility and self-confidence. We discover new meaning and purpose in our lives, which includes giving to others as well as ourselves.

Trust and faith in a Power greater than ourselves is the foundation that supports us throughout the Steps, and friendships in the fellowship give us encouragement and sustenance. We become accountable in all our relationships. With forgiveness, humor, gratitude, and kindness, we begin to live one day at a time, with joy and hope a daily part of our lives.

Stories of Hope is not designed to be read from cover to cover. We suggest that you select a topic you want to learn about and read just one or two essays to inspire you for the day. The essays can be used as the topic of discussion for your CPA meeting. The stories on these pages offer gentle suggestions, leading us to live peacefully, joyfully, and comfortably with ourselves. This is a process, an ongoing learning experience, and it takes patience. Recovery is a journey, not a destination.

May the light of wisdom in these stories illuminate the way so you, too, will reclaim hope and serenity.

PAIN

The fishermen know that the sea is dangerous and the storm terrible, but they have never found these dangers sufficient reason for remaining ashore.

Vincent van Gogh

I would like to share some concepts that I have accepted since I joined CPA.

1. Being in pain is not the worst thing in the world, but being in pain—and all alone—is the worst thing in the world for me.

2. I don't have to feel guilty about having chronic pain. I didn't ask for it. And if I had the opportunity, I would certainly get rid of it.

3. I don't have to feel less of a person if I ask for help. God put all of us on this planet so we could support one another.

4. The reason I have chronic pain is not because I am being punished by God. It is just another intricate part of existence. People are suffering all over this planet, and I could be in a lot worse state of being than I am.

5. I have always sought out adventures, and with all adventures come risk and hardship. This is just one more adventure I am having, and it, too, shall pass.

6. Pain has led me to be more spiritual and less egotistical. I have grown to appreciate the really important things in life, like relationships and experiencing moments in the present, as they are happening. I can now move into the latter part of my life with grace and dignity and peace.

7. And last, but not least, if I am having a bad day and don't want to get out of bed, I don't have to. Neither do I have to feel guilty about not doing anything that day. The world will not fall apart. Whatever needed attention will still need attention the next day, and the day after that. Maintenance is forever, so there's no rush to get it done.

Let us learn to skillfully draw good out of what would otherwise cause us harm.

ST. MARY EUPHRASIA PELLETIER

I was once fixated on my medications, dependent on them in every way—emotionally, psychologically, physically, and spiritually. In my mind, medication was the only thing that could help me. The drugs were my Higher Power. When the pain cranked way up, my first thought was "What drug can I increase next?" or, "When can I take my next dose?" I never prayed or asked God for help. Instead, I blamed God for the pain.

I'm also a recovering alcoholic/addict, and I just couldn't reconcile being an addict and having chronic pain. In my mind I was hopeless. I believed this was who I was, and it was why I would never really have a chance at recovery. I just didn't see how recovery and medication could go together. I longed for a support group where I could talk about the drugs, perhaps to convince myself, and others, that my reliance on this Higher-Power-in-a-bottle was really OK. I would explain to anyone who'd listen that I'd been abused by reckless doctors, and, as a result, was hopelessly tied to a life of pain and medication.

Then I stumbled upon CPA. I followed the discussions and noticed that the focus wasn't on drugs. Medication wasn't so much the issue here, and I was attracted to those who talked of a spiritual way of life. As I focused on their message of hope and recovery I found that my attachment to the medications, and incessant thoughts about them, seemed to diminish. As I learned to stop being a victim of addiction and pain, my life, and relationship with the medication, began to change.

One day at a time, I practice the Twelve Steps. I must practice them on a daily basis, especially when the pain is at its worst. I've learned to turn to a Power far greater than drugs. I thought I'd never think of anything but drugs when the pain was at its worst, but that has changed. Today I turn first to God for strength and comfort, and then to my program of recovery.

It has taken a few years, but I have been able to let go of some of the medications (under my doctor's supervision), and I've had to accept that I must continue to take others. My perspective has changed so much. While I still think it is important to be able talk about feelings in relation to pain and medication, in my case I have discovered that taking the focus off the drugs was what I needed most.

When you change the way you look at things, the things you look at change.

Max Planck

Someone in CPA suggested having a "Vice Day." What a wonderful idea! Now if I can just learn to shut down the voice in my head that tells me that every minute of my life needs to be productive, maybe I can use this idea to reap the real benefits of Step One. That voice so often is what gets in my way of accepting my powerlessness over my pain and illness. Those old tapes can wind up and spin like crazy, interrupting my recovery. Instead, maybe I can give myself a break.

I am "busy-ness" personified, always making sure that every moment is productive. When I wake up with a full-blown flare-up, the thought of a "Vice Day" is the furthest thing from my mind. Instead, I grab on to every bit of power I can muster, and shoulder through. Accept my pain, curl up in my recliner, eat ice cream, and read a "mush for the mind" novel? How much better I would feel the next day if I did that instead!

I'm making a promise to myself...the next time intractable pain (as opposed to the "normal" pain that is with me every day) raises its ugly head...I will choose to turn off my mental tapes and accept my powerlessness...and, eat ice cream!

I have an everyday religion that works for me. Love yourself first, and everything else falls into line.

LUCILLE BALL

When I joined CPA my thinking about my pain was very confused, in fact, my thinking about *myself* was very confused. Following the Twelve Steps has turned my life around. I no longer blame myself for my pain, nor do I make excuses for it. It is what it is—pain.

And, in admitting that I am powerless over it, which means I am not a wimp but simply a person who can't control the fact that I am in pain, I have many choices about how to live my life. Turning my pain and my life over to my Higher Power has made all the difference. I have given up the defensive struggle to be more, or other, or different than someone who is in pain. In doing this I have become more accepting of myself. I have reached out to the compassionate people in the CPA fellowship and recognized that many people struggle. I no longer am burdened by thinking of myself as less than others, and I've given up my identity as a special victim.

In spite of unseasonable wind, snow, and unexpected weather
of all sorts—a gardener still plants. And tends what they have
planted ... believing that Spring will come.

Mary Anne Radmacher

By looking at my life strictly through the lens of pain, I became
consumed by my pain-self. I was allowing the pain to drive not
only my actions and behaviors, but also my thoughts and feelings.
It was truly "all about me!" What the Steps have given me is a path
to flourishing growth that makes me larger than that small, pain-
consumed person I used to be.

Is my pain any less than before I began? Not at all, in fact it is
considerably worse. But it is no longer who I am. It does not de-
fine me. I think of myself as a mostly content and peaceful grand-
ma, who usually finds life to be a kick! And, oh yeah ... I live with
chronic pain.

My hope is that others who live with pain and illness can find
a life as wonderful as mine, with the help of those things called
"Steps," which may seem so foreign at the beginning but are so
continually nourishing over time.

If you always do what you've always done, you'll always get what you've always gotten.

JESSIE POTTER

When dealing with pain or other difficult physical symptoms, looking attractive goes to the bottom of my priority list. Tasks like showering and hair washing demand too much energy. Thank goodness for hats. As for clothes, when I was first ill I spent years living in dark-colored sweats, because they were easy to mix and match and felt loose and comfy, like pajamas. It was a good day if I combed my hair.

I see now that when I do make the effort to look put-together, even on a bad day, I feel steadier inside. As I've heard in meetings, acting "as if" makes a difference. I usually feel more confident when I have taken the extra time and energy to look presentable.

When I think of the choices I can make that will bring more serenity and peace into my life, sometimes it starts with something as simple as combing my hair.

Every loss in life I consider as the throwing off of an old garment in order to put on a new one; and the new one has always been better than the old one.

Hazrat Inayat Khan

After I lost my health, and along with it my career, friends, and family, I was sure that I would never be happy again—it would be downhill from that point on. Experiencing happiness in life was no longer possible. Period. Then I read a line in a book that changed my life. It went something like, "…pain and loss are not incompatible with joy and loving life." The Twelve Step program of CPA was my answer to the question of how one can learn to find joy again. There was much to grieve, and I had to mourn the losses. However, the past does not determine the future. The core of the CPA program is the love I receive from my Higher Power, and the faith that my Higher Power knows what is best for me. I need to surrender into whatever is happening as perfect, even though it does not look anything like what I had envisioned—this is the key.

It is something that did not come easily at first. I was angry, blaming, and resentful. I hated my body, the medical system, and all the people who were still young and healthy. And I did not want to let go of these feelings! Even though I was adding to my pain by hanging on so tightly, I resisted working the Steps and seeing my part in my misery.

My Higher Power brought me the books, people, and experiences to gently help me let go of the past and begin living in the present. Thankfully, this process is never completed. Working through the Twelve Steps with my sponsor again this year has deepened my awareness of the character defects that impede my path to happiness. It has given me more opportunities to clean up the wreckage of the past, and to learn to love myself just as I am, in the body I inhabit today.

There is a saying in Twelve Step programs, "Don't quit 5 minutes before the miracle." I used to think I could order what I wanted from my Higher Power. It is a relief it doesn't work that way, because my Higher Power has far larger dreams for me than I do for myself.

When we find God in all that we experience, in the raw and painful as well as the happy and good aspects of life, our faith matures.

Estelle Frankel

The definition of self-pity is, an exaggerated sorrow and moaning over one's misfortunes and sufferings. This would describe me, before CPA. I wanted everyone to know how sick I was, how my suffering was worse than anyone else's, and that I deserved everyone's attention and concern. Poor, poor me.

By working the Steps, I became aware of this behavior. I didn't like finding it; I felt shame about my self-pitying attitude. But I also discovered that self-pity is sometimes about sorrow. Today I am not well, and it has interfered with my life in a big way. I am angry at God, and I am angry at my body for betraying me. I am angry at the unfairness of my illness. I need some time today to grieve and to acknowledge the losses of this day. I need to remember that all I have to do today is live this day.

When my grief rises, I remember that I am not alone and that I have a Higher Power who loves me and wants the best for me. I may not like my Higher Power's idea of what the best is, but I just keep returning to the first three Steps: I can't, You can, I will let You. So I pray for willingness to surrender and to accept my powerlessness.

LOSS

When it seems humanly impossible to do more in a difficult situation, surrender yourself to the inner silence and thereafter wait for a sign of obvious guidance or for a renewal of inner strength.

PAUL BRUNTON

Grief can hit all at once as the result of a life-altering event, such as the death of a loved one. Or, it can be a relentless, dull ache of realization that life is not dealing us the hand we expected. Today I am grieving for my expectations of a life I had envisioned. A life with health, peace of mind, security, independence, a happy marriage and fulfilling career, and being a contributing member of my community.

It is hard to accept all the losses and unfulfilled expectations. I never imagined a life so hard and painful. Sometimes I attempt to deny all the changes, but then the reality of my situation hits me like a demolition ball and knocks me off my feet. I cannot ignore "what is."

In those difficult moments I realize I have my meetings and recovery friends whom I can talk to and who will understand my tangled emotions. And right by me, around me, above, below, and within me, I have my own loving, patient, understanding Higher Power, who has always been there for me.

I have faith that my Higher Power will carry me through the times when the pain feels intense and difficult. It is then that I surrender. I do not know where I am going, I just trust I am being taken to where I need to be. And I always am. My Higher Power always takes me to a greater, higher, safer place than the one I was in before, leading me further along my journey.

Grief can be the garden of compassion. If you keep your heart open through everything, your pain can become your greatest ally in your life's search for love and wisdom.

RUMI

The CPA program gives me new tools and hope. There is a way out of the agony of grief. I think this is what has kept me going when the grief felt like a heavy blanket that was suffocating me, when the losses and sadness seemed so oppressive they felt like they'd go on forever.

We are never totally done with grief when living with illness, but we can learn to trust the process and know that we will move through each loss, and there will be joy again. This is where the fellowship is so important. When I am buried under my blanket, CPA is the flashlight peeking through to remind me of the possibilities yet to be discovered, the acceptance waiting for me when I am ready.

My faith in a Power greater than myself, together with this program of spiritual recovery, always lifts the despair of grief. Eventually. I say "eventually" because that is not my starting place. For me, grief needs to be expressed first through tears and self-pity. Grief is physical for me, not just emotional. My body aches, my heart aches, every cell cries out "why?" and "this is not fair." Trusting there is a plan helps me hang on another hour, another day.

A powerful tool given to me by CPA is gratitude. I get so consumed by focusing on what I've lost that I become blind to what I have. I resist gratitude because I don't want to give up my anger or my attachment to what I am grieving. When I manage to shift my focus to the positive, I find there is quite a lot I do have in my life. And sometimes, the loss gets transformed into a new beginning— a gift, something quite wonderful and unexpected. "One Day at a Time"… one hour … one minute … I get through the period of grief. It is often not pretty, easy, graceful, or fun. There is no right way, and there is no time frame. There is an end, however. I don't like hearing this slogan when I am in grief, but I know it is true: "This, too, shall pass."

One can choose to go back toward safety or forward toward growth. Growth must be chosen again and again; fear must be overcome again and again.

ABRAHAM MASLOW

With chronic illness and chronic pain our condition does not stay the same. We get better, we get worse. We likely will have to cycle through the resulting emotions more than once. We may go through the denial, anger, and grief with each new loss. It can take several years to just accept the diagnosis. It took five years for me to accept that I was ill and wasn't going to get well.

Today I see an increasing decline in my cognitive and physical condition. It has taken me a year to decide to let go of my pursuit of a graduate degree, to release my dreams of working in a new field. I find myself revisiting grief and realize that I've been resisting it for months. I understand now that it is time to accept my feelings.

The fear is that I'll sink into a depression if I acknowledge the grief I am feeling. Then I remember that I've been here before, got through, and felt much better on the other side. I learned in CPA that feelings pass. They are messy and uncomfortable, but with my Higher Power at my side, I have faith that I will be OK. My hope may be lagging, but it will return once this emotional storm has passed.

Someone told me once that when one door closes, another opens. But you have to let the door close. Living with pain and illness, we have to close a lot of doors! I pray once again for the strength and courage to let go and surrender to the unknown.

FEAR AND ANGER

You feel the way you do right now because of the thoughts you are thinking at this moment.

DAVID D. BURNS

Since illness and pain are so unpredictable, new opportunities to feel fear often arise, and we are powerless over that happening. What we can do is respond differently than we have in the past. We don't have to run with the ball. We can set it down.

The important thing to know is that we are not alone. I find the oppression lifts when I can speak my feelings aloud to others, and get hugs and love and hear how they get through the scary times.

With the support of the fellowship, the fear may not disappear, but it decreases and becomes more manageable. With practice, we come to strengthen our ability to respond in new ways to these challenging feelings. We can take the harmful thoughts out of our minds by shifting our attention to something that brings joy and makes us happy.

When I get junk mail, I often toss it right into the recycle bin without opening it. I can do the same with my thoughts and feelings. Just because they show up does not mean that I have to open them. Sometimes fear is useful, but when I find myself obsessing over and over about all the dreadful things that might happen, I can consider it junk mail, toss it, and move on to something wonderful that is right in front of me. When I have trouble doing this, I reach out to someone and ask for help. God does a wonderful job of sending me what I need to manage my fear, every time, so that I can return to peace and serenity.

A man of courage is also full of faith.

Marcus Tullius Cicero

For many years I was overwhelmed by constant fear and worry. My doctor prescribed medications to help reduce my anxiety, and a therapist helped me with depression. I always felt so alone struggling with this problem of thoughts run rampant.

When I came to CPA I discovered that other people also experience persistent unwanted thoughts. These thoughts are like a broken record, and they are often focused on fears of everything I can imagine. There seems to be no way to control them.

Through doing the Steps, I came to have an understanding of an all-loving and all-forgiving God, and I learned that I could turn over my fears and worries to my Higher Power. I could put them in His care. And then I would feel relief.

The challenge is still to leave them there. This takes practice and patience. As long as I am willing to keep doing it, I have success. I have less fear and fewer worries. My faith in my Higher Power increases. And I begin to know peace.

Two of my favorite slogans now are: "Replace Fear with Faith" and "FEAR—Face Everything And Recover."

There's only one corner of the universe you can be certain of improving, and that's your own self. So you have to begin there, not outside, not on other people.

ALDOUS HUXLEY

For me, anger is extremely hard to deal with. When I get caught in anger, it robs me of any connection I have to my Higher Power, of any gratitude, joy, or peace. I know that it is different for all of us. I think that some people can access their anger and it does propel them forward toward positive solutions. But me, it takes into a dark, ugly place.

Part of doing the Fourth Step was exploring the role of my anger in my life. I learned that it just can't be safely contained. It works best for me to recognize the anger rising and then take action to shift my thinking. Giving any room for the anger does not serve my best interests.

The best thing for me to do is to stop obsessing over the event or person that got me angry. I need to call someone in CPA so that I can have help seeing the whole story and not just my side of it. I need to balance my perspective from being all about me to incorporating all the circumstances involved. And then I need to give myself, and my anger, over to God; to say the Serenity Prayer, asking what I can change and putting my efforts into the solution. Otherwise, I am staying focused on the problem, not the solution.

When I am ill, the worst thing I can do for myself is expend my limited energy on anger. It accomplishes nothing. With the help of CPA friends and my Higher Power, I'm gradually learning more effective ways to manage my anger.

It is a huge danger to pretend that awful things do not happen. But you need enough hope to keep going. I am trying to make hope. Flowers grow out of darkness.

Sister Mary Corita Kent

In other Twelve Step rooms, I've learned so much about fear and how to manage it. However, with illness and pain, the fear seems remarkably overpowering at times. I have found that learning how to get through periods when the fear almost drowns me is an important skill that takes lots of practice. This one shift in my thinking and actions, knowing there are options beyond being immobilized and stuck in fear, opens the way to serenity, in profound ways.

I've heard in meetings that the opposite of fear is faith. It is so true. When I return to the first three Steps, acknowledge that I am powerless, that my Higher Power can help me, and feel willing to turn myself over to my Higher Power's care, then I remember that all will be well. I can't see the big picture, but my Higher Power can, and I need to let go of the way I think things should be and let my Higher Power lead the way.

Generally, my fear is not real. I am either taking something negative from the past and projecting it into the future, or I am creating scenarios in my head about a future that likely will never happen. This is where "One Day at a Time" works so well. I ask myself, this minute, this second, am I OK? Is there a roof over my head? Is there food in the fridge? Are there people who are there to support me? If not, then I review "First Things First." What needs to change this moment to improve my situation? I remember that I always have choices. What can be changed in this moment? That is where the Serenity Prayer comes into play. Change what I can and let go of what I can't change.

Using all these tools sounds good on paper, and they work when I use them. But sometimes I still create my own suffering, way beyond the reality of the situation. This is when I call my sponsor or program friend, or pray, or meditate, or read something I know will remind me of the tools that are available. Having a CPA fellowship means that I am not alone in the fear, so it doesn't loom large like it did in the past.

I have reached a point in my life where I understand the pain and the challenges; and my attitude is one of standing up with open arms to meet them all.

MYRLIE EVERS

I denied the fear. I didn't think I was afraid of anything. Turns out I was afraid of many things, but it came out sideways. I was angry. I sank into depression, self-pity, and isolation. The fear owned me. Not only was I miserable, but everyone around me was too; I made sure of it.

Something had to give. What I was doing was not working. My life was a shambles, and it wasn't the pain that was the problem, it was my reaction to it. Clearly I was not dealing with it well. Finally my fear drove me to drink, after eighteen years sober in Alcoholics Anonymous. That's what finally woke me up.

I returned to Alcoholics Anonymous and began to work the Steps around my chronic pain and illness. Then I found CPA, and here I learned I didn't have to face my fears, my pain, or any difficulties alone. Here I have found great comfort and strength in talking to others who are dealing with the same challenges.

As I work through fear in my Fourth Step, and I put my thoughts, feelings, and behaviors down on paper, I begin to see and understand just how groundless, and at times detrimental, my fears can be. I can begin to differentiate between the positive, motivating aspects of fear, and the negative, debilitating ones. This awareness is a direct result of working Step Four, and it didn't hurt a bit!

Loss makes artists of us all as we weave new patterns in the fabric of our lives.

GRETA W. CROSBY

I used to be very close to some of my family members, especially my nieces and nephews. When I became sick, in a matter of two years they had all left my life, thinking I was faking, lazy, and whatever else was in their heads. The pain was, and still is, excruciating. I struggle almost daily with the loss of my family and close friends, who have left due to my illness and their misunderstandings about it.

But someone said something to me as I was working through the Fourth Step and my resentments towards those people. She told me to put them in a bowl full of God's love. I didn't have to carry them anymore. Now some of them I didn't want *near* God's love, but she said that surrounding them in God's love would be a different experience for each one of them, and that once in God's love, they might be able to see things more clearly. I am not going to wait around for that, but I did write all their names on paper and put them in a white bowl.

The second thing I did was even more helpful to me. I wrote down all the feelings I had about them leaving my life—abandonment, hatred, betrayal, indifference, loneliness, and anger. Suddenly I found I didn't need to carry those feelings anymore. I gave them up, put them in the bowl, and I found I had much more energy. I had no idea how all-consuming the feelings had become. By giving them up to God, I found I could do other things with my time: Read more, do more writing, spend more time in this fellowship, and enjoy other favorite activities.

I was able to do all of these things because of the fellowship I have in CPA. It has changed my life. I have found people who "get it" so I don't have to spend time explaining. They also give me help when I can't see straight, need a shoulder to cry on, or want to have a fun chat without being asked about what I'm doing with my life.

It's not what happens to you, but how you react to it that matters.

EPICTETUS

Anger and blame. Old habits I seem to lean on so naturally, as if they were old friends. However, sometimes we have to let old friends go because they are causing us harm. When I'm angry and blaming, I am wasting precious energy staying focused on the problem instead of putting my energy into the solution.

There are several questions that help me when I start to feel anger and blame. The first is "How important is it?" The second is "Are you living in the problem or the solution?" and the third "Is this serving my best interest?" And, since I know that I am not always honest with myself, I often need to call my sponsor or someone in CPA to help me come up with answers. I once heard someone say that even their delusions have delusions. It made me laugh, because I saw myself. So I get out of my head, a "dangerous neighborhood," and ask for help.

Another tool that is invaluable for me is the Serenity Prayer: *God, grant me the serenity to accept the things I cannot change, the courage to change the things I can, and the wisdom to know the difference. Thy will, not mine, be done.* This always helps me, because it reminds me that in living with illness, sometimes the only thing I can change is my attitude. Yes, I want the world to change, and my body to change to please me, but much to my dismay and repeated disappointment, I've found it doesn't work that way.

But blame and anger are not the solution. They take a whole lot of energy. I have to manage my energy, just like I manage my money—every penny matters. Just as exceeding my means by buying things with my credit card creates financial debt, focusing my energy on things I can't change creates energy debt, and then I don't have the resources left to do what brings me joy.

ACCEPTANCE

You don't get to choose how you're going to die. Or when. You can only decide how you're going to live. Now.

Joan Baez

It was very hard for me to accept my condition and the fact that I would probably never have my old life back. When I was told that my condition was chronic and the best I could hope for was that it wouldn't get worse, I almost burst into tears. *Never* get better? I couldn't even wrap my mind around that thought.

I tried all kinds of treatments. Then, one day, after receiving a new treatment of injections, I woke up in extreme pain and had to go to the emergency room. As I lay in my hospital bed, praying for God to take this pain away so I could at least roll onto my side, I realized that I had tried everything and nothing had worked. The injections had only masked the pain so I could continue working, but in the end, ignoring what my body was trying to tell me resulted in even more pain.

To me, the idea of acceptance had always meant giving in. I began to see that this was not the case. It means accepting things as they are, not how I want them to be. It means letting go of denial. Once I began to accept things as they were, I quit wasting precious energy fighting reality. I did not give up trying to improve my situation, but I was able to focus my energy on living wisely so that I would have more strength and more peace.

I may never be like I was before the accident. I have some bad days and some good days. But acknowledging my situation has made it easier for me to ask for help. Realizing that I can't do everything I used to do enables me to live in a way that is good for me and restores me. Acceptance has meant that I no longer wear myself out in futile resistance, but instead, *take care of myself.* Acceptance has made it possible for me to experience serenity.

True hope can open our hearts and remind us of light when we are in darkness. But when our hope for relief from suffering is based only on getting what we want, the precise way we want it, we bind hope to fear, rather than to faith.

Sharon Salzberg

When I was first diagnosed I believed that I would soon find a treatment, get well, and get back to my "real" life. It took years before I understood I would never be my old self again and that *this* was my life. I mourned the loss of the "well" me and became quite depressed. I didn't believe I could enjoy life with this body.

When CPA came into my life, there was a sense of relief in knowing that I was powerless. I could finally stop my constant search for the right doctor, right therapy, right medication. When I stopped trying to do it alone and surrendered my life, including my body, to my Higher Power, I began to recover.

I did not recover from my illness. I recovered from the emotional and spiritual wasteland that resulted from my illness. In CPA I learned to let go of the stories of what my life and body should look like and begin to have gratitude for what did exist. I became willing to let my Higher Power guide me.

Today I can feel happy, joyous and free. These qualities are no longer dependent on the elimination of pain and illness. To get here I had to start with embracing that I was powerless and totally let go of making anything happen. My efforts to control and manage were my obstacles. CPA showed me a new way and it starts with Step One and powerlessness.

Perhaps all the dragons in our lives are princesses who are only waiting to see us act, just once, with beauty and courage. Perhaps everything that frightens us is, in its deepest essence, something helpless that wants our love.

RAINER MARIA RILKE

I was a young woman when I first needed a cane. I cursed my pain and the cane. As a young, athletic businesswoman in the prime of life, I grieved the loss of my ability to function in life as it once was and was stubborn in my refusal to accept these new circumstances.

I fought using a cane with all my might. I didn't want people staring at me and was deeply ashamed, judging myself harshly. As a result of not using it *all* the time when it was needed, I struggled more than necessary and compensated for the weakness and pain by using muscles in other areas. Over time this caused even more limitations and pain.

Luckily I found this Twelve Step program and surrounded myself with wise, loving, and caring people. They helped me to learn to accept my pain and limitations, and have compassion for my body. This was new thinking.

They taught me to love the parts that hurt. I began to rub my leg and speak softly to it, extending empathy and kind words that I would give to a young child in pain. Instead of cursing the pain and my situation, I began to love and accept the parts that hurt.

Rather than cursing the cane I began to thank it as a loyal friend. Instead of shamefully hiding it in a corner, I began to display it as a supportive friend who loves me unconditionally. I began to use various canes in a fashionable way—a pretty one for social events, a rugged one at the beach. Now people often remark about my fashionable canes. A friend carved birds and frogs and other animals on her cane. I admired it and she suggested I join her wood-carving class. She gave me a suitable stick for carving... and, who knows.... I may become a wood carver!

Every day I have a physical reminder of how pride can't only damage my soul, but also my body. Today I choose acceptance, love, and gentleness, and I reject negativity, judgment, and harsh words. I am grateful I have a choice today.

Calming allows us to rest, and resting is a precondition for healing. When animals in the forest get wounded, they find a place to lie down, and they rest completely for many days. They don't think about food or anything else. They just rest, and they get the healing they need.

THICH NHAT HANH

Sometimes I hurry because I am afraid that if I don't get something done quickly, when I am having a good day, it may be a long time before I feel well enough to get to it again. But sometimes this means pushing myself too hard on good days and going into a relapse as a result. "Easy Does It," which means, pace yourself, is something that helps when I have that sense of urgency. Over time I've learned that things get done when they get done. They may stay on my list for months, even years, but they do get done. Or, sometimes items sit on my list and by the time I get to doing them, they have resolved on their own. My Higher Power works in mysterious ways, and not being able to do everything when I want to, ends up being a gift.

I learned in CPA that when in doubt, don't—don't act, don't do anything. This is when I rely on my Higher Power to guide me. When the road ahead looks foggy and I can't make a decision, I need to trust that the timing, information, situation is not clear yet, so just do nothing. This is when the first three Steps come into my life. I need to have faith that my Higher Power is in charge and he will let me know when to act and how. I heard at a meeting that we can't see around corners, but our Higher Power can.

This faith in a Power greater than ourselves is the core of having a program of recovery. I may not do it perfectly, but when I remember to step into this faith, peace and serenity, joy and laughter, enter my life.

Worryin' is just prayin' backward.

DAVID CHETHLAHE PALADINE

S tep One is the first of the spiritual steps. It says, *We admitted we were powerless over pain and illness—that our lives had become unmanageable.* In taking this Step I see that I am not in control. I do not have all the answers. No matter how many books I read about my illness, how many specialists I see, how many healers I contact, my life remains unmanageable.

This Step asks me to stop wasting my energy struggling to fix my pain and illness. It beckons me toward humility. Step One asks me to become aware of and begin to accept my powerlessness. I am able to see that this thing is bigger than me. I need to become truly and deeply humble and open my eyes to my place in the scheme of things when it comes to my pain and illness.

I am powerless. I don't have to seek any more answers. I don't have to try to figure this out anymore. Step One begins my journey toward acceptance, and the next Steps will lead me closer to healing and peace. The physical pain and illness may still be with me, but the emotional pain does not have to be.

Everybody is unique. Do not compare yourself with anybody else lest you spoil God's curriculum.

BAAL SHEM TOV

I had been staying sober one day at a time, and when I saw good things happening to other people who were doing the same, I began to compare my progress and my good things with other people's. And, as my physical problems and chronic pain became worse, I really started to feel a big resentment and anger towards my God. "God, I am working the program, trying to be a spiritual person, practicing spiritual principles in my daily affairs, and here you have burdened me with new problems and restrictions. Is this my reward for working the program and doing what I am supposed to do?"

My friends at meetings tell me I should not compare myself to others. So I'm doing that less and less. And I try every day to thank my loving Higher Power for the goodness that exists at my very core—the goodness that He/She created. And I pray for the courage to love and honor and respect myself, and to be grateful for all the blessings I have.

If I can do that, then I'm less likely to be envious of others and their blessings. But all this is a work in progress. I can slip at any minute and fall into jealousy. I need to ask my Higher Power on a daily basis to help remove these defects of character.

It's definitely hard not to want a body free of chronic pain, a body that can move around at will. A key to my inner peace under these circumstances is acceptance. When I accept myself and my condition, as it is, then I am much more likely to find serenity and freedom from jealousy.

Yesterday is but a dream, tomorrow is but a vision. But today well lived makes yesterday a dream of happiness, and every tomorrow a vision of hope. Look well, therefore, to this day.

SANSKRIT PROVERB

Not only do the benefits of Step One never diminish, they keep increasing. When I truly admit that I am powerless over pain and illness, then I can use my energy for living life, rather than fighting my body.

In the past I always worried about having company stay in my home. I'd be anxious for days beforehand, worrying that I'd be stuck in bed with pain and illness and unable to enjoy my visitors. This past weekend my adult daughters were home for a family celebration. For the whole week before, I found myself at ease, knowing that I am powerless over my pain and illness, and could choose to surrender to whatever happened rather than trying to control or manage it.

When I woke on the last day of the visit with a variety of symptoms, it didn't provoke an attack of insanity. Unlike years ago, I didn't immediately think, "Oh no, now this will be a terrible day." I know from past experience that pain and illness do not have to be a problem unless I give them the power to be a problem. I am powerless over what is happening in my body, but I am NOT powerless over how I choose to respond.

The pain and illness did not have to become the focus of my day, and, just as importantly, it did not have to be the focus of my family's day. I chose not to share what was going on, and went about the plans for the day. I am powerless to change my body, and when I acknowledge this, I take the attention off of my body and put it into what is happening in the moment. Like laughing with my family, enjoying a meal together, and watching a movie.

When I admit my powerlessness, I can choose to let go of controlling the pain and illness. Once I do that they recede into the background and my enjoyment of life comes forward.

The art of living lies not in eliminating but in growing with troubles.

BERNARD M. BARUCH

After many years of pain I have finally accepted that chronic pain may be part of my everyday experience. It's not that I am pessimistic or have lost my faith in miracles. Just for today I am accepting my powerlessness over my pain and my disability.

This is a major step for me. For years, no matter how bad things were, I clung to denial of my condition and to the belief this would pass and I would get better. I directed my energy into the future, where everything would be back to normal. Today I know that my normal is *what is happening now*. I stay focused on my care plan, not on what it was like before my illness.

I realize that living in the future was not a good way to use my energy. I am learning to focus only on this day. I accept what is, and appreciate all the good things in my life. I am working with my sponsor on Step One, accepting my powerlessness over the pain. I am becoming aware of how unmanageable my life can get if I try to control it. I also notice how unmanageable my life can be when I live in the past or the future.

Things are still really hard. My pain is getting worse again and my doctors say they have exhausted their options. This has been emotionally painful and difficult to accept. But acknowledging my powerlessness has shown me I can grow in faith and keep taking care of myself as best I can. Nothing is impossible with my Higher Power loving me and guiding me. I use the principles of the program to stay connected, "One Day at a Time."

The great opportunity is where you are. Do not despise your own place and hour. Every place is under the stars, every place is the center of the world.

JOHN BURROUGHS

L ife seemed unfair when I was demoted from a high-level position in the technology sector, but I was grateful to keep my health insurance. Then things got tougher when my job was completely eliminated, but I was grateful to still have my health. So when I became ill soon after these losses I had no income and no safety net. When it comes to acceptance and dealing with life not having worked out as planned, I have learned a great deal about myself and my God.

I came to realize that God was not to blame for my illness. He hadn't forsaken me. Facing surgery, I had to pray, turn it over to God, and not hold on to a specific outcome. When I work Step Three, I need to totally let go, and by doing so accept whatever the outcome may be. That is turning it over... period.

God has given me and my family a bounty of blessings. We have followed a path set out in our belief and our faith. Is my life as I had planned or dreamed and worked toward? No, it is not. In fact, in some ways it is even better than I had hoped. I have a relationship with my wife and son that probably wouldn't have been possible in my career. Are we provided for? Yes, maybe not like before, but we have more than we need.

I am so thankful to the program of CPA. Without the Twelve Steps I would never have been able to emotionally go through what life has dealt to me in recent years. I would be a mess, and probably alone. Now a Power greater than myself has actually made life better, even with the challenges that I have encountered.

A great attitude does much more than turn on the lights in our worlds; it seems to magically connect us to all sorts of serendipitous opportunities that were somehow absent before the change.

EARL NIGHTINGALE

When I first became ill, humility and surrender were two things that went against every instinct. I wanted to fight, solve, take charge, fix—conquer my illness. I was determined to triumph over it. Because of this attitude, humility and surrender were hard for me to grasp at first, and I resisted them for a long time. I thought they meant giving up, giving in, becoming complacent. I feared that if I let go of my vigilance—even just a little—I would get worse.

My sponsor asked me to be teachable and to act "as if." I was reassured that if I didn't like the results, I could go back to my old ways. This is how I was able to approach Step One and begin to see that the tools of CPA work. I dipped my toe into the waters a tiny bit, and lo and behold, something new happened. It was something good! Hey, I thought, maybe this Twelve Step stuff really does work with pain and illness. The more I applied Step One to my life with illness, the better I felt and the happier I became. I was not cured of the disease of my body, but I was healed of the disease of my mind and spirit.

But could it be just a fluke? The beauty of the fellowship is that over the years I've seen others join with the same skepticism I had, and I've seen spiritual awakenings and healing of mind and spirit, again and again. And, as in my own life, I've seen the miracles that occur when we let go and surrender, with acceptance, to God's plan.

What God has in store for us is good and far beyond anything we can imagine for ourselves. To receive, we need to become humble and surrender.

Inside of a ring or out, ain't nothing wrong with going down. It's staying down that's wrong.

MUHAMMAD ALI

Yesterday I drove to the post office, parked in the disabled parking space with room for my ramp to go out, and went to mail some letters. Upon getting back into the van, as I started up the ramp, my wheelchair started to tip back, the right tipper guard didn't work and I went over backward.

Fortunately, my training in rehabilitation helped. While going over, I grabbed the back of my head with my right hand and tucked it into my chest, keeping my head from being the first thing that hit the ground. So I was sprawled out on the pavement, feeling helpless and alone. My work with the Twelve Step program kicked in once again. I quickly took inventory of myself, thanked God that I was conscious, and sought and found my glasses. I worked at rolling myself from my right side to my back and reached to find my wheelchair. I wondered if I should yell out for help? I didn't, because I had faith that the right people would come, in God's time, to my aid.

Sure enough, a man yelled as he ran toward me, "Do you need help?" I replied, "No, I just love lying on the pavement in a busy parking lot." We both laughed and discussed how to best get me back into the chair. He helped me get back into the chair and up the ramp and asked if I needed to go to the hospital. I felt I didn't and drove home and took care of my new aches and pains.

The next day I awoke feeling better, with some new pains to again turn over to the God of my understanding. I will go about my life as I am right now, sharing the wonders of this Twelve Step program. That is how I go about acceptance, and it works for me. I pray, as I do each day, that others will find the grace in their life that the Steps and recovery have given to me.

When you accept one hundred percent responsibility for your experience, you gain one hundred percent of the power to create the experience you would choose.

ALAN COHEN

In my recovery from chronic pain, the most important piece of the puzzle was acceptance. When chronic pain began to overtake my life, I withdrew from my family and stopped going to my other Twelve Step meeting. I became quick to anger, driving away those I loved. Depression set in for the first time in my life, and I saw no hope or future. This was a dangerous place to be for an alcoholic. Doctors told me the only solution would be narcotics. So I was left to choose between my angry pain state or one that made me feel groggy and drugged.

Through the Twelve Steps of CPA, I have been able to see that there is a third choice, one that allows me to rejoin the human race. One that allows me to contribute to myself, family and friends, and society. I am no longer a taker; I am now a giver. I am someone who, through love and compassion, can stand tall in any environment (even though I am in a wheelchair). I am able to be a mentor and father for my son, a husband for my adorable wife, a son to my aging mother. I live each day with honesty, humility, and respect for all in my life.

The key to all of this is the acceptance of my pain. Some days it can be difficult. Nonetheless, by accepting reality, I can take total responsibility for everything that happens in my life.

Acceptance allowed me to turn to God. Then I was able to seek out doctors I trusted. I could look at alternative means for my recovery. Having done this, I was free to choose, with a clear and educated mind, and be a full partner with whichever health provider I was working with. Even with chronic pain, life is manageable.

Go outside, to the fields, enjoy nature and the sunshine, go out and try to recapture happiness in yourself and in God. Think of all the beauty that's still left in and around you and be happy!

ANNE FRANK

My pain has been increasing over the last few weeks. This morning when I awoke, it was unbearable, and I received no relief from my medications. I began to panic when the pain did not subside. I jumped to all kinds of negative conclusions about the future. But then, before falling into the emotional pit of paralysis and fear, I took a deep breath and said one short prayer: "Help."

After I had paused and began feeling calmer, it became apparent that the overwhelming rush of feelings was the result of self-pity. I had been making plans for what I wanted to do with my life—go back to school and find a job. The reality is that my future is unclear and my plans may not be possible. It is uncomfortable acknowledging that I have little control over what the future holds.

I have been here before, and I learned that I gain peace when I let go and accept God's plan. Mourning any loss is natural, but I see there is a very fine line between mourning and self-pity. The main difference is that grief is part of the process of moving forward and letting go, while self-pity can keep me stuck in the past.

The gratitude for all that *I do have* was buried under the self-pity. The little improvements I had been ecstatic about just a few months ago, I was now taking for granted and my gratitude had disappeared. A lack of gratitude seems to grow into self-pity.

I will choose to keep my focus on today—not next month, next year, or even tomorrow—and have gratitude for all my blessings.

TRUST

When a man is willing and eager, the gods join in.

Aeschylus

L iving in a body can be such a trial. It doesn't always hum merrily along. Some people who have good health think it is because of something they did right and that if you live with pain and illness, you somehow did something wrong. They think that, until they get ill and experience pain. And it will happen. No one gets through life without physical disease and pain. Bodies break down, whether from disease, accident, flawed medical care, genetics, or old age. It's a natural progression.

Right now, aging is my latest challenge. It is adding more pain and taking away cherished pleasures. When I woke the other day with multiple pains due to multiple causes, I was not happy. I ranted, raved, yelled at God, swore at God, decided the Twelve Steps are useless. Yet I know that the only way out is through. I have to embrace all my feelings—fear, grief, rage, frustration, disappointment, despair, sadness, disillusionment. I am powerless to change the situation or to be anything other than human, with a full range of emotions and thoughts. The difference between now and before CPA is that I cycle through the emotions and negative thoughts in minutes, rather than days, weeks, or months.

The other day a CPA buddy was caring and supportive when the feelings were drowning me. She listened without judgment or the need to fix me. I've learned that my Higher Power does not abandon me and is far bigger than any emotion I may have. This, too, shall pass. Maybe it will be after some sleep, a good meal, a hug, a smile from a kind person, a walk in nature, but inevitably, however it happens, life will look good again. Though there are times when the road to my serenity goes through a dark alley, I've learned God never lets me go into those dark alleys alone.

And God is always there, if you feel wounded. He kneels over this earth like a divine medic, and His love thaws the holy in us.

St. Teresa of Avila

Step Seven: *"Humbly asked Him to remove our shortcomings."*
In the past, when I had perceived shortcomings in myself, I'd figure it was my responsibility to get rid of them. I'd see a therapist, read a book, talk to friend. I would never even consider prayer. I was sure that I could do it alone. I did not see how God could be of any use.

Humility is a thread that runs through the Twelve Step program, which means developing an understanding of our place in the universe. I always had a tendency to think I was the center of the world, and illness merely reinforced this delusion. I subconsciously believed that it was everyone's job to make me happy by behaving in the ways that I am most comfortable with. I acted as if everyone should know my needs were important. This applied to strangers as well as family and friends; their job was to do what I expected so I would be happy.

The CPA Twelve Step program has helped me become aware of the many ways in which I had to take responsibility for my thoughts, words, and actions. I began to develop humility, seeing my place in relation to God and other human beings. After I became humble, I was ready to ask my Higher Power for help. I don't have to know how this will work. All I have to do is follow the directions.

Sometimes God removes shortcomings immediately, and other times, years later. I wake up one day and another one is gone. Sometimes they fade away gradually, sometimes not at all—but God somehow uses them for good. God is always there, bringing me the people, the books, the experiences I need so He can remove my shortcomings. We are all a work in progress!

Whoever does not see God in every place does not see God in any place.

RABBI ELIMELECH

It amazes me how my Higher Power, whom I call God, continues to provide what I need. As I seek and am willing to heal, God keeps dropping things in my lap. This gives me much-needed clarity and direction about a lot of feelings and thoughts regarding my health.

I often get very confused and fall into the blame game. I waffle between blaming others and myself for my health and pain—mostly myself. Either I can't understand why I have pain and want the doctors to give me an answer, or I blame my lifestyle and myself for my condition.

Today I mentioned to my neighbor that I was having a pain-filled day. She offered to help me with my laundry and bring over dinner. Rather than going down the well-worn path of shame and belief that I am unworthy of her concern and efforts to help me, I tried something new and said yes. It brought ease into a difficult day. It was a new experience to stop seeking someone to blame, merely accept the situation for today, and receive kindness from someone who cares about me.

What I am starting to see now is that I'm responsible for a lot of how I feel about my situation. My core beliefs have to change. I have always felt that I was not worth anything, was unlovable, and no good. But my Higher Power has been showing me that I am good, I am okay, and I am lovable. I see that I no longer have to hold on to all those old painful hurts and resentments. They are no longer needed and I'm done with them, I'm moving forward to better health, acceptance, and wholeness.

Although we have been made to believe that if we let go we will end up with nothing, life reveals just the opposite: letting go is the real path to freedom.

SOGYAL RINPOCHE

When I came into CPA from another Twelve Step program, I had already developed a relationship with a Higher Power. However, I didn't trust that my Higher Power could truly relieve me of the insanity I was in, from living with chronic pain and illness. As I began to practice Step Two in CPA, new possibilities for healing were revealed.

For me, this Step works in three parts:

"Came to believe"—I open my mind to a different way of thinking. I am willing to see through new eyes.

"...that a Power greater than ourselves"—I understand that there is something in this Universe greater than me; I am not alone, and there is help when I ask for it. I am free to discover this Power for myself. I can use a familiar belief system and build on it, or I can explore a new one. When I attend CPA meetings I listen to members share their experience, strength and hope about their Higher Power, and this offers me new insights.

"...could restore us to sanity"—I become aware that my thoughts and feelings are not peaceful and even sometimes irrational. When I notice this, I pause and ask my Higher Power to restore my sanity. I then believe that my Higher Power can and will do so.

In practicing Step Two I acknowledge I don't have all the answers, nor do I even know all the questions. As I surrender myself to my Higher Power it becomes clear that I can't find my way to serenity by myself. I am not alone. My sanity and peace of mind can be restored. What a relief! There is the possibility that I will love my life, and there is hope for a better today.

It may be that when we no longer know what to do, we have come to our real work, and when we no longer know which way to go, we have begun our real journey.

WENDELL BERRY

This is a fluid program, always moving us forward. For some of us, the loving spirit of our Twelve Step group may be our Higher Power. We use this bond we feel with others in CPA to help us see ourselves, and to help us change some of our unpleasant behaviors. It is so much easier to do, and more effective, if we use that spirit which unites us with others who live with chronic pain.

This process of recovery has become much easier for me since I realized that I'm not finished yet, and probably never will be. And that's a good thing. It means I don't have to be perfect...not on my first swipe at the Steps, nor on my thirteenth in-depth study of them. There will always be room to grow. Gradually I am incorporating the Steps and this new way of life into every nook and cranny of my being.

Believe more deeply. Hold your face up to the Light, even though for the moment you do not see.

BILL W.

Step Three states, *"Made a decision to turn our will and our lives over to the care of God, as we understood Him."* Some of us are not ready to act on this immediately. We need to first consider the *possibility* of making the decision to turn our will and lives over to a Higher Power. In time we take the leap and make a decision.

Over time we begin to act on this decision. We test it out, slowly. We may give over one decision to our Higher Power, and then another. As we notice ideas, people, and solutions falling into place, we learn to trust that this process is working.

We give over a single problem, such as whether to see a specialist or not. Then the phone rings and it is a friend saying she just saw a new doctor for a similar problem and he helped her. We wonder if God is guiding us. So we try it again.

Step Three unfolds over time. As I turn over more and more of my will to a Higher Power, I notice that my life gets richer and fuller, regardless of the pain and illness I may feel. I don't need to know how this works—just that it does. As I heard in a meeting, "Life is a joyous adventure and a mystery to be enjoyed, not a problem to be solved."

I find it liberating, peaceful, and comforting to turn my life and my will over to the care of a Higher Power who is kind and loves me. It is clear that my own efforts only took me so far. My powerlessness limits what I can do, as I learned in Step One. My Higher Power's guidance has brought changes in my life that I could never dare imagine before CPA. In practicing Step Three I am shown how to invite my Higher Power into every area of my life, including my pain and illness.

FAITH

Happiness cannot be traveled to, owned, earned, worn or consumed. Happiness is the spiritual experience of living every minute with love, grace, and gratitude.

DENIS WAITLEY

I have lived with chronic pain and illness for a long time and struggled alone during most of those years. Although I attended all kinds of support groups, often all I heard was hopelessness and despair. I had enough of that on my own, thank you very much. I didn't need more. I did not know there were possibilities for living a different way than one focused on suffering and loss. I did not have the benefit of hope and experience that I have now found in CPA.

There were many years in which I had my suicide note ready. Many years that are a blur of pain, sadness, and isolation. It wasn't until I came to CPA that my life began to turn around. The people in the fellowship have given me hope, shared their faith in a Higher Power with me because I had none in the beginning, and told me to keep coming back because the program works.

In CPA the Steps and tools of the program are like a flashlight highlighting the path out of the dark tunnels of suffering, and into lightness of spirit, toward joy and serenity. This beacon of light begins with a Higher Power who loves us, wants the best for us and hasn't abandoned us.

Today I choose life ... again and again. This precious human life, even on the days when my body does not feel like a friend, is a gift I treasure. I can make my life whatever I want. It is up to me to enjoy it or hate it, so I might as well make it a life I love. In CPA I have finally come to understand that I can't change my body, but I can change my mind.

I pray that each person living with chronic pain and illness can feel the love of a Higher Power for the beautiful and perfect person they are today. I pray they can surrender the past and begin to count the blessings of today. I pray that sharing my experiences with the Twelve Steps can illuminate the path, so that another person doesn't have to wander alone in the darkness and be lost for as many years as I was. I am here to support others, and I am here to be supported. We are all in this together.

People, even more than things, have to be restored, renewed, revived, reclaimed, redeemed; never throw out anyone.

AUDREY HEPBURN

When I came to my first Twelve Step meeting, there was no Higher Power in my life. I was in despair and had lost my hope, my confidence, my joy. This was the end of the line for me. If it didn't work, I promised myself that I could take my life. I thought the whole Twelve Step thing was rather dopey, but I chose to give it a try. I had nothing to lose.

I found a sponsor and worked the Steps. It worked, and eventually the dark clouds lifted and I found my enthusiasm for living again.

When I arrived in CPA after my first Twelve Step recovery program, I was skeptical. I knew that the Twelve Step program worked but wasn't sure that it would really work for my pain and illness. After all, despite many years of trying to fix my illness, nothing had gotten better. It had even gotten worse. Could God really handle this one?

I soon learned that just like in other Twelve Step programs, when I am willing to find a sponsor and work my way through the Twelve Steps, I change. And when I change, my entire world changes.

My real problem was my obsession with my illness and with myself, and the fact that I made sure that everyone in my life joined me in this obsession. CPA is a program of spiritual recovery. Along the way, if it is part of God's plan, aspects of illness can be lifted. Not always in the way we imagined, but when we get out of God's way, there are infinite possibilities available, beyond our limited, controlling minds.

When we accept what is, get out of self, and turn our life and our will over to the care of God, we become instruments of service, and miracles happen.

Recovery can occur in the most unlikely ways.

God is at home. It's we who have gone out for a walk.

Meister Eckhart

It is 1:15 AM and I'm just about to go to sleep. My pain is up, and when it gets almost intolerable, the way it is now, I begin to wander around my house, almost aimlessly, forgetting why I'm going anywhere and unaware of what I want. As I was doing this just now, I remembered my Higher Power and thought, how about if I just pray?

What struck me then is that I often forget to pray, and I often forget my Higher Power. This understanding is nothing new. I've known and remarked on this before and have heard others say the same thing, but what feels new is I suddenly understood that the pain makes me forget my Higher Power, just as it makes me forget everything else in its wake. It virtually obliterates my reason, my desire, my hope, my ability to think clearly. I have been down on myself for forgetting my Higher Power, but now, it is so clear to me that remembering is, in itself, a gift of God. Not something I can will to happen. I have heard others' anguish about their inability to remember to turn it over; like, "what's wrong with me?" I think the pain is what is wrong...and any respite we can get from it, even enough to think, "I will pray, I have a Higher Power to turn to," is, in itself a miracle.

Now that I have remembered and turned it over, I am noticing that I am breathing differently. Not holding myself quite so tightly, letting my shoulders sag and my stomach soften. Making room for my Higher Power to be close enough to help me.

God always provides what we need, but we must be ready to open our eyes and see it.

MIDRASH

Part of powerlessness for people with chronic pain involves the loss of dreams. After I'd been ill and in bed for over a year, I realized that I had to turn my most precious dreams over to God. I felt that chronic pain had stolen them from me. There was a lot of grief involved in this surrender.

A couple of years later God brought a new friend into my life. I had no idea how powerfully God would use him to bless me. God gave me a new dream, and we started a CPA meeting together in our community.

We prepared for our meetings in my friend's empty rental home. It had remained empty for months despite actively trying to rent it out. It was another situation in which my chronic pain friend felt powerless, and it was causing financial hardship for his family. My friend and his wife and I continued to pray that God would show them what to do with the house.

Then God gave us an amazing new dream: to turn the house into affordable, short-term housing for patients needing extended medical care. We wanted to extend to them a warm, comfortable, home-away-from-home, and our friendship along with it. My friend and I had been tremendously affected by the wonderful people in our lives during the most serious parts of our illnesses. Now we could do the same for others.

One of the most amazing things about this new dream, for me, was that it was one of the dreams I'd relinquished to God. He had rewrapped it and returned it to me when I was truly ready for it!

When I remember the Serenity Prayer, *"God, grant me the serenity to accept the things I cannot change, the courage to change the things I can, and the wisdom to know the difference. Thy will, not mine, be done,"* I have hope that God will show me the dreams that can still be lived out, even with chronic pain.

Scars remind us of where we've been—they don't have to dictate where we are going.

Joe Mantegna

The Steps are done slowly, one at a time. Step Six is not asking me to turn over my defects of character. It is just asking me to be open to the possibility that they can be turned over and removed. Removed not by me, not by my therapist, but by my Higher Power. I don't have to do all the heavy lifting.

I used to think that I had to solve every problem by myself. Step Six reminds me of something I learned in the first three Steps: that I am no longer alone. I can't, God can, I will let Her.

I have my list of character defects, but it is not my job to treat them like a list of errands to complete, checking them off as I go along. All I need in this Step is awareness of what is getting in my way of recovery and a willingness to turn myself, and all my defects, over to my Higher Power. I must remember that my Higher Power works on Her schedule, not mine.

I've been in a relapse. This time around, a few of my defects had less presence and power in my life. God has not decided yet to remove them entirely, but as I saw each one rise up, like a storm cloud over my head, I would ask that it be removed. The pressure I felt building was eased by my Higher Power in ways that I did not plan or expect. Without thinking about it, I found myself less harsh with myself and those around me. Books fell into my lap that had the perfect words I needed to hear so I could live in serenity "Just for Today." A family member helped me out financially. Each day my Higher Power reminded me that She was there at my side.

Step Six is a gentle way to ease into action through working my program, which rests on the spiritual foundation of Steps One, Two, and Three.

When you are open to Mystery, there is magic even in the midst of pain.

MIRIAM GREENSPAN

In the past I tried to control everything by myself. Ever since I became ill, life felt unpredictable, and I thought that if I was in charge I could manage the unpredictability. As a result of my trying to control how events would turn out, I was often disappointed by unexpected outcomes. With the uncertainties that come with living with chronic illness, my thinking began to lean toward a negative, rather than a positive, perspective. I would obsess on the problem rather than seek the solution. With my distorted views, and trying to control the uncontrollable, I became angry, irritable, and difficult to live with.

When I began to practice the principles of CPA and made a commitment to my spiritual journey, I changed dramatically. I went from living according to me, myself, and I, to living in partnership with my Higher Power. I have turned my thinking around so I see the positive solutions more readily. I spend quiet time daily asking my Higher Power to guide my thinking and bring clarity.

Today I have a connection with my loving Higher Power, whom I choose to call God. This relationship brings me peace and grows stronger every day. Over the years of daily contact with this gentle, forgiving, and understanding Higher Power, I now feel wonderment as I go through my day. I don't have to solve my problems alone. Where I used to jump in to fix and rescue, now I move out of the way of my Higher Power. I let my Higher Power give me awareness and solutions. This is how I practice "Let Go and Let God."

Faith is taking the first steps even when you don't see the whole staircase.

MARTIN LUTHER KING, JR.

Steps One, Two, and Three bring a simple shift that liberates us from whatever external cause we identify as creating our suffering. It is like teaching someone how to swim; telling them how liberating it is to jump into the refreshing coolness and glide effortlessly through the water. They can't truly understand until they take the leap and experience it for themselves.

The first three Steps, the spiritual Steps, lead us toward the water and that leap of freedom. We must choose to do it. We each do it when we are ready. Nothing can make us be ready. It is the grace of God, combined with our courage and willingness.

In CPA we discover we can be blessed with more joy, serenity, and peace. This is why all of us who have come to a Twelve Step program, for whatever reason, keep coming back. It works. All the Steps take practice, they need reinforcement from our literature, our fellowship, and our direct experience. And they require continual reminders. This is why I go to my meetings and use the telephone to help me stay connected and not lose my way.

Expect to have hope rekindled. Expect your prayers to be answered in wondrous ways. The dry seasons in life do not last. The spring rains will come again.

Sarah Ban Breathnach

In the past few months it seems that every day has brought news of a friend or relative who is facing a medical challenge. My very best friend of 53 years is dying of cancer. Talk about feeling power-less! Today, I heard of another friend who has my same condition, and is my age, and who has decided to give up and go into an assisted-living facility. Wait a minute! I'm not ready for that, am I?

I've been working for some time with a research doctor who specializes in my illness, and had high hopes for getting some relief. The result? So far, as my dear departed mother would have said, "I've been going nowhere fast, in a big hurry!" Nothing has changed except the number of pills in my pill sorter. And in spite of my very best efforts to stop the process, my body seems to be aging more each day. That same mother used to tell me that old age isn't for sis-sies, and she sure was right!

So where does it leave me? There is nothing in any of the situ-ations I've mentioned that is truly within my control...nothing. All I can do is the footwork, and leave the rest to *the God of my under-standing*. Most of the time I have a pretty good handle on what that means, and I can trust that my Higher Power, whom I choose to call God, won't abandon me. But sometimes, when the pain is really bad and I get one more piece of bad news, I waver. The best I can do at those times is to say the words, "I believe in a Higher Power. I believe I can trust that entity. I will ask my Higher Power for help."

Sometimes I have to repeat the words over and over, even though they taste like sawdust in my mouth, before the faith that underlies my life can rise to the surface again.

When my faith and hope in a Higher Power is alive and well, life is *so* much better!

It is by going down into the abyss that we recover the treasures of life. Where you stumble, there lies your treasure.

JOSEPH CAMPBELL

Yesterday I spent several hours in a closed MRI machine, which feels like being pushed inside a tomato juice can. I need scans fairly regularly, and they usually last no longer than 90 minutes. But due to allergies, I sneezed, and it took twice as long.

My fear of closed spaces makes this procedure a challenge, so my doctor prescribes medications to help me cope. As the procedure went on for the second hour I felt the effects of the medications begin to wear off. The Serenity Prayer became a song in my mind. I repeated it over and over. I lay in the darkness of the machine and soon discovered the Serenity Prayer was also a powerful medication, relaxing my body and mind.

Step Two says, *"Came to believe that a Power greater than ourselves could restore us to sanity."* This Step helped me to know that the pain in my body and the fear of being in the closeness within the walls of the machine would pass into distant memories if I just hung in there a bit longer. Yes, my life at that moment, or rather my mind, was in need of restoration to sanity. But in a short time I was rolled out and returned home. The feeling of insanity had passed, with the aid of a graceful and loving God.

If it weren't for the tools I have learned in the CPA Twelve Step program I couldn't have let go and let God as I did when the test seemed to go on and on. Once again the Steps of CPA saved my very sanity—one moment at a time—even in the face of what I once would have viewed as an impossible nightmare.

For it is when we encounter the face of the divine in our struggles and adversities that our wounds become a source of blessing. In discovering the divine hand moving through and shaping our lives, we uncover a deeper meaning to our existence. This restoration of meaning is itself a profound source of healing.

Estelle Frankel

To restore is to bring something back to its original condition. My original condition would be that of a beloved child of God. I lost that view of myself when I became ill, but today I can love myself as God loves me. I don't have to expect myself to be anything other than what I am in this moment. I can accept life on life's terms.

How did my Higher Power restore me to sanity? I don't understand it, but in the CPA Twelve Step program, I don't have to. All I have to do is be willing to show up and suit up: Work the Steps with my sponsor. Attend meetings. Read the literature.

It's like baking a cake. I don't know how raw eggs and dry flour and sugar granules and baking powder become something delicious just by being heated in the oven, but they do. I follow the directions on the recipe and it comes out just right every time. So my Twelve Step program gives me the recipe, and if I follow the directions, I have sanity every time, no matter what the circumstances. My Higher Power has removed from me all attachments to how things should look, good or bad. Sanity is being in this day only and having joy and gratitude for all that is good right now.

Sanity is also resilience, or the ability to face difficulties without losing hope or being overwhelmed. When my perspective changes from focusing on my problems to the solutions that are given to me by the Twelve Step program, I can maintain a wider view of myself and the world. I can have gratitude for all that is positive and abundant, of which there is plenty. I can turn to all the resources available and use any of them. I can have sanity, serenity, and inner strength, given any adversity, stress, or loss. Then I am restored to being a beloved child of my Higher Power.

We must not wish for the disappearance of our troubles but for
the grace to transform them.

Simone Weil

When it came to illness and pain, there was a part of me that
didn't believe that I was worth restoring to sanity, or that I
deserved to be well.

Sanity meant being open to a new and positive relationship
with my body and my illness. There was a part of me that didn't
love myself and felt like it was my lot in life to be ill and suffer. I
was afraid to believe that there could ever be anything other than
pain and misery.

My negative thinking had a strong hold on me. I had developed
quite an attachment to my victim role and wasn't sure I wanted
to give it up. Nor was I totally convinced that I was allowed to be
happy.

Sanity would mean being happy, and loving myself and life.
These had become foreign concepts to me over the years of pain,
loss, and struggle. I was quite comfortable on my pity pot and
wasn't sure I wanted restoration to sanity. And even if I dared to
hope, would it really happen? Or would I be disappointed as I had
been so many times when the doctor or healing modality or medication did not pan out?

In time, I took the leap of faith. The changes that have occurred
in my life, in my body, in my thinking, are profound. That is why I
have such deep faith in this Twelve Step program for pain and illness. It works … if we are willing to work it.

First, we have to come to believe we are powerless over pain and
its effects. Then we have to believe in a Higher Power. Then we have
to get out of the way so our Higher Power can restore us to sanity.
We are worth the effort! We are all beloved children of a Higher
Power who wants the best for each and every one of us.

The most important step in breaking free of a life dominated by stress and anxiety is to be present for what is actually happening, rather than to be swept away with our ideas about what may happen to us later.

DARLENE COHEN

I was told early on in another Twelve Step program that faith is the absence of fear... that faith and fear could not coexist. That served me well at the time, but I don't find it possible to absolutely apply it to my chronic pain.

For those of us who live in pain, there is always the question: "Will it get worse?" It's a reasonable question, and one that I believe can coexist with my faith. I have faith that my Higher Power will guide me in making decisions to avoid having my pain become worse. I have faith that when it is very bad, my Higher Power will give me the strength to handle it, without my jumping off the nearest bridge. I have faith that my needs will be met, my medications obtained, even when there seems to be a roadblock of some kind. And in the midst of that faith, my fear may continue to exist. That's OK.

It's when I let the fear take over totally and direct my thoughts, actions, and decisions that I get in trouble. When I avoid things that "might" make me feel worse until I've withdrawn from the outside world, I'm allowing fear to rule my life, and discarding the faith that I have found in this program. That still can happen, but today I know the way back up out of that well of fear. It's prayer, or calling a friend in the program, or going to a meeting.

I'm learning how to live happily somewhere on the seesaw of faith and fear, realizing, with the help of my Higher Power, a daily balance that makes my life manageable.

SURRENDER

Pray—period! Don't expect anything. Or better, expect
nothing. Prayer cleanses us of expectations and allows holy will,
providence, and life itself an entry. What could be more worth the
effort—or the noneffort?

Thomas Moore

Step Three: *"Made a decision to turn our will and our lives over to
the care of God* as we understood Him."

Making a decision to turn our will and our lives over is a core
foundation of our Twelve Step program. It is an action for moving
us toward "Thy will, not mine, be done." At first glance it may look
like we do it once, learn it, and then it is done. But that is far from
my experience.

When I was first in a Twelve Step program I thought it outra-
geous to turn over my will and my life. I didn't have a close relationship with my Higher Power, and with the slight connection I did
have there was not a lot of trust. I felt like I'd been let down many
times in the past. And now I was being asked to make this big decision and take this action of surrender. It didn't seem prudent to me
at the time.

I slowly edged into this Step. I turned over one, small aspect of
my life. I wanted to see what would happen. Over time, through
this "scientific" approach, I discovered that each time I made this
decision, the outcome of what I turned over was different than anything I had in mind for myself, and far greater than what I could
imagine.

It took many years before it became my initial instinct in any
situation to turn over my will and my life first, and then figure out
my action steps. And even today, this is a Step I have to be reminded of every single day, because it is so easy to forget. This is why I
continue to attend meetings, speak to my sponsor, and read the literature. It helps to have this Step in the forefront of my awareness.

Do not wait; the time will never be "just right." Start where
you stand, and work with whatever tools you may have at your
command, and better tools will be found as you go along.

NAPOLEON HILL

I was puzzled for years by what it says in the Third Step, to have
"made a decision" about turning my will and my life over to the
care of a Higher Power. Why doesn't the Step just say, "We turned
our will and our life over to the care of a Higher Power?" Why,
"made a decision?"

Finally I learned that this wording is used for a reason. All we
are asked to do in this Step is to decide. I believe the actual turning
over occurs as a result of working the rest of the Twelve Steps. So
for those of you who hesitate at this Step, relax, it will come. Don't
let this Step or any of the others deter you. The Twelve Steps are a
process, not an event.

I alone can do it… but I can't do it alone.

<small>ANONYMOUS</small>

My surrender, these past few weeks, has been daily, even hourly. I fought for so long to do it all myself. Then I discovered that the only time the pain wins is when I *don't* surrender. Every time I try to push past it and do whatever, because "doggone it, that pain isn't going to win," I find myself in much worse shape.

The key for me to is to recognize that surrender does *not* mean, quit or give up. To surrender is to do a realistic evaluation of where my pain is at any given point in time, and decide if I need a little help to get through whatever is in front of me. Surrendering to reality doesn't mean I stop doing everything and expect others to care for me. It just means that I no longer set my expectations of myself so high that I'm unable to see when I'm hurting myself.

My biggest struggle is that I am so darned stubborn...and that's where a belief in a Higher Power comes in. I pray for the willingness to see my pain realistically. And then for the ability to ask for help, be it physical or mental or spiritual, when I need it.

There is little danger that I will become a whiner and complainer, because my pride is so strong that I still don't want to admit, "I can't." Many times I dig in and just push through the pain, only to suffer later. Occasionally, when I ask my husband for help with something, he'll give me a look that says, "What took you so long to ask?" He tries very hard not to rob me of the ability to make the decision to ask for assistance on my own and so doesn't jump in to help prematurely.

For me, the power in surrender is that I can maintain my dignity, while allowing others to participate in my pain struggle...and it always feels better when I do that. Now if I could just remember to do it every time!

I have woven a parachute out of everything broken.

WILLIAM STAFFORD

Many of us who deal with chronic pain and chronic illness must eventually turn to some form of medication. Each of us responds to this in a different way. For those who have led a particularly healthy existence, focusing on exercise and organic food, it is disheartening to accept that we must now allow chemicals into our bodies. We might be overtaken by panic that these medications are too expensive, or that we may become addicted. Some of us have past addiction issues, and fear overwhelms us. Sometimes we find ourselves coping with foggy brains and fatigue, the side effects of what has been prescribed.

These difficulties must be accepted, right along with our illness and pain. The Twelve Steps of CPA can help us overcome the feelings, however powerful, that accompany the need to take medication, even though we might not realize it at first. Applying recovery program principles works with all aspects of our condition, including the use of medications for relief of ongoing pain and illness treatment.

For behind all seen things lies something vaster; everything is but a path, a portal, or a window opening on something more than itself.

ANTOINE DE SAINT-EXUPERY

Surrender is liberating. It does not mean giving up. The image I have is being on a mountain, struggling to find every handhold and foothold, but never making it to the top. And then I surrender, let go; I fall back, into the arms of my Higher Power.

Surrender is choosing to do things in a different way, turning it over to my Higher Power instead of trying to do it by myself. I let go, and then I open to infinite potentiality. Once I achieve that, anything can happen. In a sense, my Higher Power has effortlessly placed me atop the mountain. I'd struggled to climb—and failed— all by myself. It was in my limited thinking that I stayed hanging onto the struggle.

With my mountain image in mind, I realize that in this moment, I am OK. I find gratitude and let go of future outcomes. This was hard at first. Never one to ask for help, I was used to doing everything myself. Surrender opens the door for new possibilities.

Thro' many dangers, toils and snares, I have already come; 'Tis grace that hath brought me safe thus far, And grace will lead me home.

JOHN NEWTON

When I first became ill I was not in a Twelve Step program, so I thought that surrendering meant giving up in defeat. I spent many years and many dollars searching for answers so I could get rid of my pain and illness. I was not willing to accept my situation as it was, even though the results of all my efforts were dead-ends and an empty bank account.

Since my experience in other Twelve Step programs, and now CPA, I understand what it means to surrender. The definition is: "To give oneself up to the power of another." This is the core of the program, the first three Steps, to accept my powerlessness, come to believe in a Higher Power, and turn my life and my will over to the care of that Higher Power.

When I first became ill I took pride in my ability to fight, to not give up, to march forward no matter what. And I think this attitude has a time and a place. During the acute and early onset periods of illness and pain, we need this inner warrior. But after years and years of chronic pain and chronic illness, we need some new tactics.

Now when I think of surrender, I do so with a sigh of relief. Finally, I can let go. It was so exhausting to hang on and fight for so long. One of my favorite sayings is, "If the horse you are riding on has died, get off." Steps One, Two, and Three showed me how.

The irony of surrendering is that once I did stop trying to force solutions and gave myself up to God's guidance, my life changed. In part, I had been contributing to my suffering through my own self-determination and fierce independence. I had to reach my personal bottom before I was willing to let go and truly surrender to my Higher Power. Today, as my symptoms flare, I am grateful for the reminder to "Let Go and Let God."

Security is mostly a superstition. It does not exist in nature, nor do the children of man as a whole experience it. Avoiding danger is no safer in the long run than outright exposure. Life is either a daring adventure, or nothing.

HELEN KELLER

Step One: *"We admitted we were powerless over pain and illness—that our lives had become unmanageable."*

I fought for many years, seeking answers and trying to get well. It wasn't until I surrendered to being powerless over pain and illness that I was finally liberated. I had always thought that I would be giving up if I accepted the pain and my powerlessness. It turned out to be just the opposite.

Working the First Step allows me to stop trying to fix my life, and start living it. This Step makes it possible to let God into my life. It brings new possibilities that I, in my desire to control everything, had never allowed. It keeps me from being the victim, who believes the world is a cruel and unfair place. In owning my vulnerability and need for my Higher Power's guidance, I can stop whining, and I am empowered with the discovery of all the ways I can create a peaceful and happy life.

Before I found Step One I was a person who managed everything and believed I did it well. I was terrified of letting go of the slim thread of control I thought I had over my life with pain and illness. With Step One I learned that control was always an illusion, even when I wasn't experiencing pain or illness. In examining what I truly had control over in life, I discovered very few things. Certainly not other people, not the weather, not the government. Really, nothing much outside of myself, and even that was questionable.

This Step was the first on the road to getting out of God's way, becoming humble, being teachable and open to the miracles of the program.

Always be ready to remind yourself that healing is a process, not a single event. As on a long train ride, the journey is most enriching and enjoyable when we learn to relax and watch the scenery, leaving the "driving" to God.

LINDA NOBLE TOPF

I didn't believe surrendering would really work for pain and illness. I was sure that my Higher Power would not be able to change anything. When the alcoholic in my life made me feel angry I could leave the room. If I had an obsession with chocolate, I could just not eat chocolate. But pain and illness? No way. They went with me wherever I went. All the doctors and treatments couldn't help me. It was hopeless. Nothing worked, and certainly my Higher Power didn't care, because he allowed this to happen to me in the first place.

There was much emotional energy bound up in controlling every aspect of my life. I was afraid that making the wrong choice, be it what I ate, what I wore, how long I stayed out with friends, the medications I took, going to a noisy mall, exposure to chemicals, would bring more pain or symptoms. My fears of making things worse, of not controlling my life perfectly, took much joy out of living.

Recovery is a continual process of letting go of my obsession with my body, my pain and my illness, and living each moment with acceptance of whatever is happening. Since every hour, every day, is different, I need to keep returning to Step One.

I found that the more I let go of controlling, the more energy was liberated to be open to life-affirming experiences. The more I surrendered, rather than always trying to fix and manage my body, the more I was open to the love and guidance of my Higher Power. Beyond anything I could imagine for myself, my Higher Power brought healing from suffering in ways that were unexpected.

Surrendering into complete acceptance opened the door for my Higher Power to work in my life. This made it possible to begin to thrive, no matter what my body was doing on any given day. Step One seems counter-intuitive at first, yet once one gets the hang of it, it is life-changing.

We tend to judge ourselves for our mistakes and the difficulties we have experienced, when it is the difficulties that build our character. You are far stronger for what you have gone through.

ALAN COHEN

Step Two: *"Came to believe that a Power greater than ourselves could restore us to sanity."*

In the beginning of this chapter of my life I had no idea that a Power greater than myself could restore me to sanity. I only knew that I was in pain and I still had everything to do—go to work, clean the house, grocery shop, babysit grandchildren, participate in family functions, bicycle, work out at home with weights, and everything else entailed in daily living. Yes, I was hurting, but all of this stuff still had to be done, right? The idea that it did not have to be done never entered my mind.

The insanity for me was the desperation to keep up with everything, fulfilling everyone's expectations, the guilt for not doing so, the grief that I could not, the fear for what the future would hold, the shame of letting people down. When I found CPA, a whole new world opened up to me. A world with hope for a good life in spite of my circumstances, and with tools for practical application: for emotional and spiritual balance, and serenity. I learn over and over again that my Higher Power can restore me to sanity.

When things are overwhelming, sometimes I remember to ask God to take this moment, this day, and to show me what He wants and what is best for me. I turn the day over to Him and rest in the knowledge that He is in control and what needs to get done will get done, even if it is "just resting." This brings me closer to sanity and farther from frustration and pain.

When I am feeling strong and the pain is low, I want to do more. I also need to turn these times over to God and ask for His wisdom. If I don't, I get caught up in the insanity of pushing too hard, and end up paying for it with an exacerbation of my symptoms.

I am very thankful for the continuing learning process about my Higher Power being able to restore me to sanity. As time goes on I am getting a little better at asking for His help sooner rather than later.

Everything comes to us that belongs to us if we create the capacity to receive it.

RABINDRANATH TAGORE

The "Three A's: Awareness, Acceptance, and Action," are tools of the program I use when I find myself struggling with pain, weakness, and low energy. Before I force myself to push through an uncomfortable situation, I pause and consider how to apply these tools. This helps me to refocus my energies.

I've always been one to fight the good fight and just keep pushing through bad times, telling myself tomorrow will be better. But today I have the *Awareness* to recognize when this approach simply isn't working for me. Sometimes, when I am in a relapse, I can't do the things I would like to be able to do.

With the awareness of my limitations, just for today, I can begin to find *Acceptance* and let go of the fight. When I accept this is how it is right now, I can let go of unrealistic expectations and surrender to God's plan for this day.

With God's guidance, I know what *Action* to take. I am kind to myself. I put aside my to-do list and focus on what I need most— rest. There are quiet activities I can do, such as reading or watching interesting programs on television. I can sit outside in the nice weather. Just for today, I can "accept the things I cannot change."

My prayer is a simple reminder of how to apply CPA tools when I'm lost. "Please help me to accept what is; to surrender to Your will, with gratitude and humor."

COURAGE

Have courage for the great sorrows of life and patience for the small ones; and when you have laboriously accomplished your daily task, go to sleep in peace. God is awake.

Victor Hugo

The very first thing that comes to mind when I think of Step Three is the way it is written. It calls for us to make a decision to turn our will and lives over to the care of God, as we understand Him. It doesn't tell us we must take the action that minute. It doesn't tell us how to do it. It only asks that we make the decision—that we be willing.

Those of us who have worked these Steps in our lives, with addiction as well as with chronic pain, know that the sooner we are able to actually take that action, and give our will to God's plan, the more quickly we will find peace and relief from our emotional turmoil. But for anyone who is still struggling with the God concept—who hasn't decided exactly what *"God as we understood Him"* means—this Step offers the possibility that we may find some relief just by making the decision to try it at some future time.

The second thing essential to working this Step is to realize that we may often need to reaffirm this decision. I find myself making this commitment daily—the higher the pain level, the more often I repeat those words. I have a picture in my head of what it looks like when I turn my will and life over to that Higher Power. I visualize one of those little wooden paddles, which has a small rubber ball attached by a long rubber band. The object is to hit the ball up, again and again, and catch it with the paddle every time. In my mental picture, the ball is my will and my life... I hit it hard, way up to God.

Sometimes I see that ball in my mind's eye staying up, and know that my Higher Power is completely in charge. But the times when I take that ball back, thinking that if only I fight this pain hard enough it will go away, are far more frequent.

This reminds me that I am truly a work in progress. Please be patient, I tell myself, God isn't finished with me yet.

When we persevere with the help of a gentle discipline, we slowly come to hear the still, small voice and to feel the delicate breeze, and so to come to know the presence of Love.

Henri Nouwen

Applying the gentle discipline of the Twelve Steps, using the slogans, and regular contact with my sponsor, I feel prepared for any medical challenge.

I hadn't been feeling well for a few days, and knew the discomfort was not associated with my chronic medical problem. I had no idea what was wrong and I felt fear and panic. I practiced "Easy Does It" by being kind and compassionate and giving myself permission to rest and relax.

As the pain grew more severe I became scared. This is where the CPA recovery program really kicked in. I practiced Step One and acknowledged my powerlessness. My connection with my Higher Power was strong and I knew I was not alone. I practiced Step Eleven and meditated, which helped me feel more relaxed and centered. I found that when I stayed present in the moment, I was calm, and the pain was not as intense.

I felt vulnerable, but I didn't run the old tapes of self-pity and identify as a victim. I discovered that God gave me the strength and courage to do what I needed to do. I went to the doctor and I felt my Higher Power was with me. I did the footwork and let go of the outcome. I believed that all was going to work out perfectly when I "Let Go and Let God."

With medication to treat this temporary illness, the pain began to subside. A day later I was resting in the comfort of my bed and began sobbing, releasing all the fear and sadness that had been building up. Unlike the past, I did not suppress the tears. I have learned in CPA to trust my body and not fight it.

Working the CPA program of recovery once again transformed a frightening experience into one of spiritual and personal growth. Working my program does not prevent me from having health problems arise, but when they show up, it gives me the tools that I need to navigate with confidence and courage.

In me it is dark, but with you there is light;
I am lonely, but you do not desert me;
My courage fails me, but with you there is help;
I am restless, but with you there is peace.

DIETRICH BONHOEFFER

Taking medications is slippery ground for everyone, with and without addictions. We all have our own ideas about taking any medication. It ranges from those who unquestioningly follow doctors' orders, trusting completely in their physician's judgment, to those who see modern medicine and all drugs as evil and unnatural. Most of us probably are somewhere in between.

I no longer have to trust my own thinking, or that of anyone else. Whether I take a drug or not, or pursue a new form of treatment or therapy that has risks, some of the worst pain I experience is the emotional pain. The fears provoked by the "what if's"—the worries about cost, the concerns about what others may think and about how it will affect my family—all of this noise in my head quiets when my faith in God's guidance is strong and leads the way.

When I am deeply connected to my Higher Power, any decision I make is the perfect decision—even if my decision needs to be altered and revised along the way. It is all part of God's plan for me. Sometimes the path is murky, and that is part of the plan as well.

There is no right or wrong answer. We all do the best we can with what we have, but we do have choices. My world of hope and possibility expands infinitely when God and I are on the same team, and I am not all alone making those choices.

I believe that men are here to grow themselves into the best good
that they can be.

JOHN COLTRANE

As a person in recovery with chronic pain, if I live according
to the Twelve Steps of CPA, then I am living a life that is
accountable to myself, God, and my fellow man. It is a life worth
living.

To live with honor and integrity, I must be honest with myself.
I have to be able to look in the mirror without feeling guilty. I must
engage with others in daily life and be available emotionally and
intellectually. I must both listen and respond.

This past weekend a fellow member in CPA called to talk. I
was tired and my mind was elsewhere … it wasn't with the call. We
all have those moments and must forgive ourselves. It's OK. I can
apologize if necessary. It is all part of learning to do the right thing.

Today while at the mechanic's garage I wheeled my chair outside where some people were taking a smoke break. Our conversation came around to why I was in a wheelchair, as it usually does.
How awful it seemed in their minds. I told them it wasn't that
bad if one were able to accept reality. We can't control the cards
we are dealt in life, but we can control how we respond. Well, our
group of smokers and nonsmokers started to grow as the conversation moved into being responsible for our lives and accountable to
ourselves and others. I don't think many of these men and women
often engaged in this type of conversation. Before I started talking
there was a lot of complaining. After I got involved, that mood
changed … it was a lot of fun!

On most days I would have watched TV or read a book while
waiting for my car to be serviced. Today, somehow, I chose to go
outside with those being shunned for their bad habit. By being
available to others, I took what I'd learned in CPA out into the
world.

To be alive in this beautiful, self-organizing universe—to participate in the dance of life with senses to perceive it, lungs that breathe it, organs that draw nourishment from it—is a wonder beyond words.

JOANNA MACY

Fear of what others think is such a big issue, with or without illness. One of my favorite Twelve Step sayings is, "What you think of me is none of my business." Another favorite saying, and this one applies to those of us who are ill and live with "invisible" disabilities, is, "Don't compare your insides with another person's outsides." I know that there are times I work hard to look well put together when I go out to social events, and someone there who does not know me may be thinking that, judging by the way I look, my life must be much better than theirs. I know because I do this when I see other people, and then when we begin talking, I learn that my new acquaintance was up all night with a migraine headache, or is recovering from a mastectomy for breast cancer. I am reminded once again that we are all human and we all suffer as the result of having bodies.

My fear grows large when I get caught up imagining horrendous scenarios of my illness getting worse in the future and worrying that my friends and family will judge or reject me. Program teaches me to return to this day and live it to the fullest. Though this is not always easy to achieve, it is a great formula. As I strive to follow it, the moments get better all the time. This shift in attitude gives me hope for a new kind of future, one in which I am free to be exactly myself in *every* moment, without fear, worry, resentment, or longing.

ACCOUNTABILITY

Not being able to govern events, I govern myself.

MICHEL DE MONTAIGNE

Working the Steps and a program of recovery is all about accountability. For a very long time I expected everything outside myself to fix me. I expected doctors to do it, or drugs, or treatments, or surgery. And I was miserable because none of the things *they* did worked. My misery showed up as anger, fear, blame, self-pity, isolation, depression, and spiritual bankruptcy. It wasn't long before my emotional pain equaled my physical pain, and those around me began to suffer right along with me. In all honesty, I had become a pretty pathetic individual.

Then, in desperation and utter defeat, I began to reach out for help in a new direction. I knew from my previous involvement in Alcoholics Anonymous that the Steps could work on just about any obsessive behavior. So I began to work them with a focus on chronic pain. And through this work I began to take responsibility for my suffering. I became accountable for my thoughts and actions. That's what the Steps are all about—taking ownership of the things I do and the way I live.

Living with chronic pain doesn't mean I have the right to make others suffer. I'm accountable for what I do and say. If I lose patience with my children, it's not up to the kids to just let it go because I am in pain. It is up to *me* to be responsible for *my* impatience and *my* cranky mood. Working the Steps helps me see how pain has influenced my thoughts and actions. Once I become accountable, it's difficult for me to continue with the same thoughts and behaviors that were once a way of life. Now I try to take each day as it comes and to be the best person I can, especially in times of severe pain.

The mind is its own place, and in itself
Can make a Heaven of Hell, a Hell of Heaven.

JOHN MILTON

In CPA we talk about the emotions and feelings that prevent us
from living as full and happy a life as possible, within the parameters of our various disabilities. Someone shared in a meeting
and used the word obstacles, rather than defects or liabilities, which
got me thinking. I've always loved dissecting words, and my first
reaction to obstacle was that it meant something in my way, that is
outside of myself. The word itself comes from the Latin for "stands
in front of."

Obstacle is defined as "something that obstructs or hinders
progress." So, true, that could be something outside of myself, but it
could also be something within, like fear, or anger, or shame.

An obstacle could be a decision of the healthcare system regarding our care. Our angry or resentful *reaction* to that outside force is
the obstacle within us that prevents us from moving forward, and
that impedes our progress.

Why all this discussion about a simple word? I guess it's because it gave me a new outlook. The words defect and liability have
always had a negative connotation for me, but an obstacle sounds a
bit more like something I can work toward preparing for removal
by my Higher Power.

The simplification of life is one of the steps to inner peace. A persistent simplification will create an inner and outer well-being that places harmony in one's life.

PEACE PILGRIM

One thing that I appreciate about the Twelve Step program of CPA is that we learn to break down our actions into manageable pieces. For instance, Step Eight doesn't tell me I have to make any amends yet. It just suggests I think about whom I would make amends to, and become willing to make them. This plan of action, one little bit at a time, I can manage to do, with the help of my Higher Power.

In working this Step, I was also surprised at this little piece: I knew that when I was in pain I was often not nice to my family members, but I hadn't even considered that I was not nice to myself either. This was a revelation. One behavior I became aware of was the voice that jabbered in my head. I would speak to myself in a way that I would never speak to anyone else in my life—in a harsh, critical voice that never held back words of anger, shame, or disappointment. When I was in pain or fatigued, this voice would often find a way to kick me.

What a joy to realize that I could bid good-bye to this unkind voice! Thus I found Step Eight is a gentle way to continue the journey of healing and recovery, which sometimes means uncovering hidden patterns of thinking and behavior.

I also heard in meetings that it's useful to make three lists of persons I've harmed—those to whom I can make amends now; those I might be able to make amends to, down the road a ways; and then those folks I can never imagine making amends to, because I lack the courage or have too strong a resentment. Well, then time passes, the program and my sponsor and CPA friends work their magic, and I find that even the most "difficult" amends become quite doable.

Beginning today, treat everyone you meet as if they were going to be dead by midnight. Extend to them all the care, kindness and understanding you can muster, and do it with no thought of any reward. Your life will never be the same again.

OG MANDINO

Today I feel poorly. When I feel this way I tend to treat everyone around me poorly, including myself. I want to blame someone or something for the fact that I feel so badly. But what to blame? Am I feeling this way because I socialized yesterday, or because I ate cake last night, or because of the rear-end accident from last week?

I want to blame my less-than-kind words and behaviors on my pain and illness. This way I can be absolved of responsibility for my nasty tone of voice toward the person in line who annoyed me today. When I feel this lousy I want to be excused for my irritability and get a free pass to act any old way I want.

However, I have learned in the program to ask myself, "How does this serve me?" I find that being angry and indulging in my crankiness hurts me more than it hurts anyone else, keeping me stuck in being unhappy. And it pushes people away when I need them most.

Bad things will happen from time to time in life. And my first reaction has always been to assign blame. With the CPA program of recovery, I can do things differently, even if it means acting "as if," to move myself forward.

Just for today I will not blame anyone or try to create explanations for things that can't be explained, and I will enjoy each moment to the best of my ability.

If the past is unredeemable, and the future unpredictable, what more practical course is open than to safeguard the present by constant remembrance of the divine?

PAUL BRUNTON

What do I do when destructive emotions and thoughts threaten to overpower me?

The other day I was in the doctor's office. He casually made a comment that I experienced as unkind. Immediately I was overtaken by feelings of anger, sadness, and a desire to lash out. Before I came to CPA I would have rushed into self-righteous reaction, yelling and attacking the doctor, damaging a relationship that was a significant aspect of my medical treatment. But now, since I have gone through the Twelve Steps with my sponsor, the way I relate to others when I feel hurt is different.

Instead of acting on my feelings of hurt, I paused. Then I focused on inhabiting my body and remaining fully present. First, I noticed the sensation of the soft cushion of the chair supporting my behind. My feet were solidly planted on the floor. I was aware of the rising and falling of my chest as I breathed in and out. This was my meditation, taking a few seconds to be still, quiet, and aware of the intense energy flowing through me.

In my mind I reached out to my Higher Power in prayer. "Please guide me, give me the words to speak. Make clear what I need to do next." Wherever I am and whatever is happening, there is always the opportunity to ask for help, to request knowledge of my Higher Power's will. I am not alone.

In only a minute I was able to calm the storm inside me. As the result of the amends I made for the times I had reacted out of anger, I knew there were ways to manage my feelings that I would not regret.

The resulting conversation I had with the doctor surprised me. He told me the feedback I gave him would benefit all his patients and he thanked me for speaking up. In my program of recovery I had learned new behaviors, and it made a real difference.

Your past is not your potential. In any hour you can choose to liberate the future.

Marilyn Ferguson

Step Ten: *"Continued to take personal inventory, and when we were wrong promptly admitted it."*

Once I completed the Steps leading up to this one, I had cleared up a lot of wreckage from the past. But that wasn't sufficient, because I am human and make lots of mistakes. The way to stay current with my program is to work Step Ten. This is how I continue to keep my side of the street clean.

Not only am I human, but I have pain and get tired easily, and that is often when my ability to cope with the everyday challenges of life is compromised. When my symptoms are frequent and intense, tasks that normally are no big deal seem overwhelming. This is usually when the tone of my voice gets sharper, impatience shows up, and my emotions take over. Words come out that I regret.

I learned in Step Four that I'm accountable for my words and actions, even when I feel poorly. Step Ten makes it possible for me to repair mistakes so I can move forward with love and respect, for myself and others. It is a Step that brings me back to where I started in Step One...humility...without blaming or shaming myself.

In the past I would get angry at myself for losing control, and would be burdened with guilt and remorse. The gift of Step Ten is that now I fairly quickly become aware when I do or say things that I regret, I promptly admit it, and let go. I don't have to carry around a heavy bag of past misdeeds.

To me, Step Ten is a daily, even hourly, opportunity to be human, to err, and to make adjustments as I go along. It reminds me that I am a work in progress. When I make a wrong choice, there is room to start over, make a new choice, and grow as a person.

To open deeply, as genuine spiritual life requires, we need tremendous courage and strength, a kind of warrior spirit. But the place for this warrior strength is in the heart.

JACK KORNFIELD

S tep Ten, *"Continued to take personal inventory, and when we were wrong, promptly admitted it,"* is critical in helping me stay up-to-date with my program. The question is not whether I will err (since I am human), but when. I once heard at a meeting that recovery is a journey, not a destination. This Step helps me stay true to my recovery.

I haven't felt well the last few days and some pains have appeared. My old thinking showed up: "I can fix this, I am all-powerful, I have all the answers." Step Ten reminded me that I tend to try to do everything myself. After talking with my sponsor, I knew it was time to admit where I was confused, phone the doctor and pray to my Higher Power for strength, guidance, and clarity.

The Tenth Step is a lifesaver for me. I get reminded to keep my square of personal space nice and tidy. And since storms blow in, and other people's messes spill over into my square, and sometimes I get tired, confused, or lost and make my own messes, the program has this built-in system for maintaining my daily serenity.

I have a loving partner, and in the discomforts of the last few days, I had thoughts and behaviors that I wanted desperately to blame on him. Because of the Tenth Step, however, I knew that I had to stop looking for someone to blame for my attitude and take responsibility for myself. I could see how my pain and fatigue alter my mind and make it so easy to fall into blaming thinking.

Thankfully, this Step helped me to catch myself before I created a scene. But I know that if I had, it would be OK, too. This Step makes it possible for me to accept myself as a human being and remember that when I do err, I can repair the situation.

It's not your partner's job to be more loveable. It's your job to be more loving.

BARBARA DEANGELIS

My current relationship is fairly new. Recently I've had some physical challenges and setbacks, and I had a morning of being despondent and angry. My boyfriend was on his way to work and didn't have time to comfort me. When he called from the office, I told him how miserable I was. His response was uncharacteristically cold and unsympathetic.

I thought to myself that despite our positive history thus far, my worst fears were coming to pass—that no one can handle living with someone ill. I felt abandoned, unloved, unseen, and not understood. I started to get angry at him. After all, I was already angry at God and my body, I might as well put my sweetheart on the blacklist as well.

Then my program kicked in. I remembered how helpless people feel when they can't do anything to alleviate the suffering of those they love. I remembered the character defects that show up when I am feeling poorly. I remembered Step Four, and took my inventory. I moved the focus back onto my side of the street, which is where I have at least some control. I made amends to myself for projecting negatively into the future.

When we spoke later in the day, I made amends to my partner for thinking the worst of him. In the past, I would have spent all day angry. When he returned home in the evening I would have expected more of the same lack of compassion. Instead, I said that I understood he was feeling helpless during my health challenge. He was able to speak about his feelings and how he didn't know what to do or say, and withdrew as a result. The Twelve Steps made it possible for us to feel closer, rather than farther apart, during a difficult time.

The things I have learned in this program led me to a more positive and helpful way to respond to my feelings and my partner's. I did not create more wreckage to clean up. This is a new experience for me, and it showed me that even with pain and illness there is hope for real love and intimacy.

...I had come to understand one redeeming and heart-lifting truth: that we can always begin again. So we leave behind failure, neglect, inadequacy, resistance—we let them go, step into the present moment, and begin again.

SANDY BOUCHER

Step Eight: *"Made a list of persons we had harmed, and became willing to make amends to them all."*

When I took this Step formally with a sponsor, I wrote a list. After reading through it, my sponsor gently reminded me that two people were missing. She suggested I add God and myself to the very top of the list.

Surprised, I listened to her reasons. During low places on my life journey, there were times I had felt abandoned by my Higher Power and expressed anger at Him, essentially turning my back on this crucial relationship. I wanted to make amends by again including my Higher Power in my life, *even on the bad days.*

Amends to myself were needed because I often had harsh, unrealistic expectations for my own behavior. I was often not kind to myself, and I needed to make amends so I could have a healthier relationship with the person with whom I spend the most time.

The willingness to accept responsibility for one's own life is the
source from which self-respect springs.

JOAN DIDION

There are many simple and gentle ways to make amends to
those we have harmed in the past without doing any further
harm to them or others.

For me this is an ongoing process. In making amends to my
daughters I made verbal apologies for being emotionally and physically absent when they were growing up. My Higher Power brought
the perfect opportunity into my life, right after I had started dis-
cussing this Step with my sponsor. My daughters started the conversation, and I recognized it was the moment to make my amends.
Since that time I have been making living amends to them by not
repeating my old injurious behavior.

Over the holidays this year, I made amends to myself by going
out to eat and not wearing myself down shopping, cooking, and
cleaning. I could enjoy my family without getting cranky and adding to my pain by using up all my energy preparing and serving a
big meal.

One morning last week, I woke in deep pain and fatigue and
realized that I had played hard the day before and needed to pull
back. I told my daughter that I needed some time to myself to rest.
At first she was miffed and felt rejected, but we talked, and I explained that I really needed to take care of myself.

Her old reactions to mom not being there for her had kicked in
at first, then she recognized that and went her merry way. For my
part, I was able to kindly state what I needed, rather than yelling,
"leave me the heck alone!" and locking myself in my room, as I had
sometimes done in the past. These are my continuing living amends
to myself and to my children. What a great relief this new way of
life is for all of us!

When every situation which life can offer is turned to the profit of spiritual growth, no situation can really be a bad one.

Paul Brunton

Step Four in CPA was a turning point for me, and, it is never completed. Just the other day I was not feeling well, and I found myself being short and impatient. When my neighbor was asking me for help with something, I could feel the tightness inside my body, the curt tone of voice, the irritation being expressed in the words I chose. I knew I was being a tad rude, yet once again, I thought I had a good excuse because I was in pain. The CPA *One Day at a Time* bookmark suggests, "Just because I am in pain, doesn't mean I have to be a pain."

These old habits get rooted in deep, and they don't want to be pulled out. Thankfully, we have other Steps as the solution for dealing with those unpleasant aspects of ourselves we discover in Step Four. I had enough awareness to catch myself and shift my attitude, and the way I related, when I spoke to the next person I encountered.

This handy little excuse of pain and illness as a justification for being less than kind or responsive is one that I discovered when I did my first Step Four inventory, and it likes to pop up to this day. I'm grateful for a program of recovery which teaches me I have a choice about how I behave, no matter how miserable I may feel, and that I can change direction at any time.

Suffering is the sandpaper of life. It does the work of shaping us. Suffering is part of our training program for becoming wise.

RAM DASS

Looking ahead to Step Four, my feelings were somewhat negative. It seemed like a lot of unpleasant work, very time-consuming. I pictured it as me, finding out all of my defects.

Looking back, however, I see it as a very helpful and positive experience. Even though I am now up to Step Eight, Step Four still remains active in my life. Step Four was just taking a look at and seeing who/what I was, the good and the bad. I discovered unexpected areas that needed attention, and I'm grateful that these things were exposed, because dealing with them is improving my life. I also discovered unexpected strengths that help me to feel good about myself.

It is amazing that I can now become aware of areas that need improvement on a real-time basis. Today I often notice when defects are popping up in my life, and I can make a choice to behave or think differently, right on the spot. When I am feeling more pain than usual, or more fatigue, and it goes on longer than I am prepared for, instead of becoming depressed or fearful and letting those feelings take away my serenity, I notice them and can choose to do something about the situation. I can accept the circumstances and turn the day over to my Higher Power, whom I choose to call God, and ask Him to help me to have the best day I can have under the circumstances. I can turn my fear over to Him also. If I were not aware of my inclination to fall into feelings of depression and fear, I would not have the opportunity to handle it differently.

I find that Step Four continues to be worked, even though I have technically finished it and moved on. Doing Step Four has given me an opportunity to continue to work on my weaknesses, with God's help, and at the same time be aware of my strengths and of my progress.

The whole idea of compassion is based on the keen awareness of the interdependence of all these living beings, which are all part of one another and all involved in one another.

THOMAS MERTON

Tradition Four: *"Each group should be autonomous except in matters affecting other groups or CPA as a whole."*

I got to wondering how this Tradition applies to CPA, and my life. Tradition Four is about balancing between unity and independence. We need to tend to our own self-interests, yet also be sensitive to the group as a whole.

The Tradition tells us that each CPA group makes many of its own decisions. The group decides when and where to meet, how to open and close meetings, whether to serve coffee at the meeting. But then there are aspects of the meeting that relate to CPA as a whole, such as the use of approved literature. If each group decided to read whatever they wanted, the essence of the program would become diluted, or splinter off in many different directions. Then the whole would be affected negatively, so we willingly agree to study and discuss approved literature, which is determined through a group conscience of the fellowship as a whole.

How about in my personal life? For me, it means that my opinions don't need to be the same as those of my friends and relatives. I can respect their different views. We can be autonomous. It means that I need to take care of my own needs, but not so much so that I become selfish along the way. This is the challenge when living with chronic pain and illness. We want to safeguard our bodies, but sometimes we tend to go overboard, asking everyone around us to accommodate our needs, but not being sensitive to their needs as well.

I have learned I can take care of my needs in a way that also considers everyone's needs. I have learned how to be flexible and turn to my Higher Power, praying for guidance in when and how to speak up and when to be quiet. In praying for help for all of us, since we are all God's precious children, I can find ways to live that honor my autonomy and allow me to live in harmony with others.

We must be willing to get rid of the life we've planned, so as to have the life that is waiting for us.

JOSEPH CAMPBELL

For me, unmanageable meant trying feverishly to control my life of chronic pain and chronic illness. I was trying to keep up with all my responsibilities: job, housework, grocery shopping, family get-togethers, exercise, social life. The more I did, though, the worse my physical condition became. I put pressure on myself not to let people down. This included earning income for my family and being involved in the lives of family and friends. There was an unending cycle of more to do, resulting in more pain, resulting in the need to rest, resulting in guilt, because I was not fulfilling my responsibilities and letting people down, resulting in more pressure from myself to perform, resulting in shame.

There was also the unmanageability of trying to find a reason or a cure for my health problems. I eagerly read everything about my condition and tried many suggestions, only to spend money and energy and end up disappointed, still in pain, frustrated, worried, depressed, and confused. None of this helped.

Admitting that my life had become unmanageable simply came to mean that it was what it was. No matter how much I kept trying, the situation did not change. I could see that all of my striving was not helping, so I began to quit spending my life in this way. I learned to accept the circumstances, relax, and to change how I thought and what I did or did not do. I learned that it is OK to take care of myself and treat myself like a loved and valued friend.

As I began to live in this way and slowly learned from the literature and tools of CPA how to have a changed attitude and just do the next right thing, my life began to change. I now live a slower life, and this gives me less stress, activity, and often less pain. Of course, some times are more difficult than others, but seeing how unmanageable my life had been, made it possible for me to begin to take steps to truly improve it.

STRENGTH

Everyone has inside of him a piece of good news. The good news is that you don't know how great you can be! How much you can love! What you can accomplish! And what your potential is!

ANNE FRANK

Yesterday I woke up feeling absolutely miserable. My pain level was way up. My energy level was way down. And I felt as if a train had hit me during the night.

As the day progressed, I found myself full of negative thoughts: "I'm getting worse," "I can't stand living like this," "I'm useless to my husband." No one was giving me any indication that *they* felt that way about me. It was just the committee in my head. My husband suggested I "go rest and take it easy."

Self-acceptance, for me, is knowing that I am faced with living in pain, accepting that, but not giving in to the impulse to let it take over. I took a new approach yesterday. I read some CPA literature. I began working on restoring an old photo for my daughter-in-law. And I prayed. I asked for strength to get through the rest of the day. I acknowledged that feeling lousy for the day seemed to be within the parameters of my Higher Power's will for me at that point in time. And I remembered the Eleventh Step and asked for the *"power to carry that out."*

By the end of the day, there was little difference in how my body felt. But my emotional state was back to the me who had self-respect and positive self-esteem. The key is that to fully accept myself, I must recognize my true worth and not get lost in pain-induced negativity.

Circumstances do not make the man, they reveal him.

JAMES ALLEN

Recently I was going through old file boxes and came across things I wrote during the early years of my illness. It was evident that I had struggled for a long time about who to reveal my feelings to, what to tell them, and when.

When living with pain and illness were new to me, my whole life revolved around my health. My body and my illness were 95% of who I was at the time, and I told people about it—often. Working the Twelve Steps changed that for me. Slowly, over time, I stopped creating my life around my illness. I realized that I am not my pain. I am so much more. Pain and illness are in the background of my life today, and so take up only 10% of my awareness. They haven't gone away, but my attention has shifted.

If and when it is relevant, I share something about my pain and illness, and it is not a big deal. It's part of a much larger me, and not the focus of my attention. If I can't go out at night, and it is important someone know why, I explain. But if not, I don't gratuitously offer the information.

What you think of me is none of my business. When I met my husband I did not agonize over telling him I lived with chronic pain and illness. I had fear, yes, that it might be a deal-breaker, but I had learned in CPA that illness is part of me, *not all of me*, and if he rejected me on that basis, then I didn't want to be with him. I learned in CPA that first I have to accept me. Then, it didn't matter what others thought.

This is not something that happened overnight. It is the result of living the Twelve Steps in CPA and trusting my Higher Power to guide me, one day at a time. I can't do this alone, and the Twelve Steps are a program of progress, not perfection. I am grateful to those in CPA who do have recovery and show me what is possible.

Every being is an abode of God, worthy of respect and reverence.
Hindu Scripture

Looking as well as I can and dressing nicely has worked itself into my daily life. Up until I did treatment recently I would wear the same clothes three or four days in a row. But then I remembered my dear mother saying when I went away to school, "Be sure to put on clean underwear every day, because if you end up at the hospital you don't want them seeing dirty underwear." So I transformed that into the rule that I had to clean myself up every day. I even shaved every day. After years of wearing suits and dressing up and shaving every day for work, my way of rebelling once I became disabled was to have a goatee and be fashionably unshaven. But for the fine people at the hospital, I began shaving in addition to cleaning myself up, and wearing clean clothes every day.

They say if you want to change a pattern in your life, practice a new behavior for 21 days and that will become your new habit. Well, that is what happened to me. Dressing well and maintaining personal grooming is my new pattern. In addition to changing the way I look, it also changed the way I feel.

I began feeling good about myself every day. It felt uplifting to be clean-shaven, to not smell, to put on cologne, to dress up as best I could. I bought jeans and nice slacks to replace my sweatpants. It just somehow felt good to look good.

Today I am off to the dentist and left the house looking the best I could. For me it all goes back to the Twelve Steps of CPA. We look for progress, not perfection in how we live. Cleaning myself up, though being a paraplegic, is an integral part of my working the Steps.

Nothing will ever be attempted if all possible objections must first be overcome.

SAMUEL JOHNSON

Over the years I have faced what have seemed to be insurmountable problems. Sometimes, with very little sleep, I have been lying in bed wondering how I will even get up, much less face these huge obstacles. There are a few tools I have learned which have helped me get started when I feel so paralyzed.

I was taught early on in recovery to break things down into small steps when I get overwhelmed. A tool that has been very helpful is what I call the "one elbow technique." I say to myself, "You don't have to get all the way out of bed, just get up on one elbow and think about it for a minute. You can lie back down afterwards if you want to." Once I am resting on one elbow for a few seconds my head clears and my attitude changes. I don't feel so overwhelmed. I have broken the inertia that is my biggest obstacle.

I've discovered that this tool can be used in many situations. All I need to do is break any huge task or problem into smaller and smaller steps until I find one that is small enough so that I can take action. Any action will do. "Move one muscle," or, "Change one thought."

Another extremely helpful tool is to put a smile on my face while I am meditating, and then, as I am breathing in, imagine that I am breathing in loving, healing energy. When I breathe out I imagine I am radiating the loving energy out into the world. With this I can generate a wonderful feeling of love, connection, and beauty even if there are painful, scary, or overwhelming challenges in my life.

These tools can be used throughout my day. I practice the smiling and breathing love when I'm at work, going for a walk, or whenever I remember to do it. The really amazing part is that I can do this anytime, anywhere, no matter where I am or what is happening around me. I have been using these tools for years, and they continue to work.

We shall not cease from exploration
And the end of all our exploring
Will be to arrive where we started
And know the place for the first time.

T. S. Eliot

Step Five: *"Admitted to God, to ourselves and to another human being the exact nature of our wrongs."*

If you haven't worked any of the Steps, Step Five can appear rather unpleasant. How many of us look forward to a discussion with someone else on what we consider to be our shortcomings? If, however, you have been working the Steps with a sponsor, you may sense that this will not be as bad as it sounds, because you have already experienced the grace, understanding, and wisdom of your Higher Power and your sponsor in previous Steps.

I found that some things I was burdened with guilt over weren't character defects after all, but instead were natural and reasonable reactions to circumstances in my life. I had been hard on myself over some things that I should have been kind to myself over. Admitting what had shamed me allowed the light and wisdom of my Higher Power to wipe it away. This brought new understanding and acceptance, and relief. Other character defects were listened to with understanding and without judgment, and with encouragement to become willing to have God remove them in His timing.

I am so glad that I have done this Step! If I hadn't, I would still be burdened unnecessarily with shame and guilt. Instead, by exposure to light and truth, my shortcomings no longer have power over me. I am free to move on to take the next Steps on my path in recovery.

It's not denial. I'm just selective about the reality I accept.
CALVIN & HOBBES

I have not surrendered. I am still in the stage of looking everywhere for a solution or a cure. I tell myself that I accept the new pain and limitations in my life, but I'm still striving to find the "answer." I still try to do my job at work, and do it well. I work at being in my children's lives and my grandchildren's lives. I work at being a good partner for my husband. I am apologetic that I can't do what I used to do and achieve what I used to achieve. On one hand, I'm working on changing some things in my life in order to accommodate my new situation. On the other hand, I'm trying so hard to be what everyone I know expects me to be, and more.

I want to cry and yell at everyone, "Don't you see how hard I'm trying? Don't you see that I hurt and that I'm tired, but I'm still doing a good job?" Surrender sounds like a wonderful relief, but at the same time, it doesn't. It sounds like giving up and being weak.

It's easier for me to accept this situation personally, but it is so much more difficult to see my loved ones also having to bear the changes and not receive from me what they have in the past. I don't want them to have to adjust just for me.

Coming to CPA has given me a small ray of hope, maybe not for restoration of my physical self, but for serenity. I have a new perspective on surrendering. Maybe serenity is a small step closer than it was this morning.

All things are possible until proven impossible—and even the impossible may be so, as of now.

PEARL S. BUCK

I had become very depressed on my ride home from work. My pain was great, I was revisiting thoughts of perhaps applying for disability, and once again feeling humiliated that I can't "carry my own weight," financially or otherwise, in my home. Even babysitting my grandchildren is a problem. On top of it all, I was worrying about one of my sons who is going through some personal troubles. It seemed that nothing was going well in life.

Then I recalled something I heard at a meeting yesterday and my spirits were lifted up. On the topic of faith, a fellow CPA member said that nothing is wasted, and God has a much greater vision than we do.

It is very calming to recall words of strength and faith while in the middle of a challenge. Yes, God does have a greater vision than you or I. He knows all, we only know a little bit. Why do we slip back into projecting negative outcomes into the future? It's because we are human, and we are not perfect. But we are making progress; we need the wisdom and strength and courage we get from each other in CPA. We are God's gifts to one another.

ATTITUDE

The trick is in what one emphasizes. We either make ourselves miserable, or we make ourselves happy. The amount of work is the same.

CARLOS CASTANEDA

Living with pain and illness, I am making adjustments all the time. I've had to make compromises and give up many familiar comforts. My usual thinking is "enough adjusting already—I want life to be easy"—no pain, plenty of energy, wake up in the morning and be able to walk to the bathroom with ease. I want a body that works well and doesn't make some days so trying.

I like the program saying about the insanity of "going to the hardware store to buy a loaf of bread." It ain't gonna happen. I will be frustrated and disappointed, again and again. Just for today, I need to let go of wanting things to look different. Just for today, I surrender my desires and preferences. Just for today, I stop expecting that I can control the world and make things be the way I want them. It is all manageable if I remember I have to make these "just for todays" real in my mind and spirit.

It's a relief to let go of trying to fix my life and make all my desires come true. I can relax and adapt to this moment. I may not like it, but it's not changing anytime soon, so I might as well adjust. Fighting reality does not make it go away, and only adds to my misery.

Rather than trying to change what's happening and control the external world, I make the changes to my internal world. It often seems that when I do this my creative juices flow and new ideas pop up. I've made room for my Higher Power to step in.

If we are not responsible for the thoughts that pass our doors, we are at least responsible for those we admit and entertain.

CHARLES NEWCOMB

I used to believe that during my healthier periods, my life was going along on course and there was purpose to it. When I relapsed, I believed everything was wrong and I was a failure. Today I believe it is all part of my Higher Power's course and that all is perfect, even when I am in pain or in bed all day.

My symptoms have been in high gear the last few weeks. I've tried for years to be able to stay sane during these times. In this last wave of pain, I realized how unkindly I think of myself when I am not feeling well. I tell myself that I am defective, that my life is worthless because I spend my days in bed, that no one could love me this way. The belief that I am useless exists only in my mind, not in God's eyes and not in the eyes of those who love me. It is clear that my negative thinking exacerbates my physical condition.

Even though I have a strong connection with my Higher Power, when I become ill I move away from God, not toward Her. I get lost in my pain and suffering and forget that God is there. Little by little, through the help of the fellowship and the tools CPA provides, I am learning to move toward God, even when my symptoms are actively present. Feeling my Higher Power beside me while I am ill, I am able to detach with love from the negative voice in my head. I am able to be kind and compassionate and loving toward myself, and learn to be my own best friend, instead of an enemy.

When you feel that you have reached the end and that you cannot go one step further, when life seems to be drained of all purpose: What a wonderful opportunity to start all over again, to turn over a new page.

Eileen Caddy

Many years ago when I first became ill, my brain stopped working. I forgot how to do math, I couldn't remember that green was go and red was stop, and I couldn't organize my thoughts to accomplish simple tasks like emptying the dishwasher. I would walk into the kitchen and cry in frustration.

When I started to crawl out of the acute period of illness and loss, it was very hard to get back on the horse and care about exercising my brain. It was so easy to say, "why bother?" I didn't expect to work again, I believed I'd never achieve another goal, and it took too much energy to use my brain.

With nothing more to lose I decided I might as well make the effort, and began taking baby steps. One of the activities recommended to me was crossword puzzles. In the early months, I never finished one and had to look up the answers when they arrived in the paper the next day. I stuck with it and eventually could complete a puzzle on my own, and, much to my delight, after a while, was able to do it in ink!

I have found that there is a sense of pleasure and triumph in strengthening my mind, whether through puzzles or reading books that require me to concentrate and focus. It has nothing to do with earning money or proving my self-worth. The reward is in the simple happiness that comes from mastering something new or completing a difficult puzzle. There are small joys to be found in each day, no matter how weak I may be feeling or what my pain level.

It is so easy to give up continuing to grow when we are ill and in pain, often home alone for long periods of time, and feeling we are not productive members of society. It was easy at first to make the excuse that I was sick and in pain and I had no choice but be a "loafer." When we are willing to do something different, many unexpected gifts find their way into our lives.

Adversity has the effect of eliciting talents, which in prosperous circumstances would have lain dormant.

HORACE

A few years ago I was forced to leave a job due to severe health problems, and soon after had to let go of my apartment because of my reduced income. Right before moving out of the apartment, the relationship I had been in ended. Soon after this blow hit me, my ex-wife called and informed me that I would not be able to see our little girl anymore. This was the final straw. It felt like everything that I valued most in life had been ripped away from me. Everything but the program, that is.

These painful circumstances pushed me to start really leaning into the program. I regularly wrote gratitude lists, and it dawned on me one day that I could do what I now call a "reverse gratitude list." Instead of listing the things that normally are considered good, I began listing the things that seemed bad, but then listing the good that could come from these seemingly "bad" things.

I began to realize that I had gained humility and acceptance by letting go of the job. I gained a relief of a financial burden, along with humility, from letting go of the apartment. I learned more compassion and acceptance in losing the two relationships. Once I was able to look at these events, in hindsight I could recognize how I had gained from each one of the experiences. I had grown in a number of areas by going through pain and difficulty. These are not things that can be learned by reading a book or by taking a class. They only come through experience.

Now that I have gotten in the habit of doing this reverse gratitude list, I've discovered it helps me find the positive when life gets rough. It doesn't change the situation; it changes my attitude about it, which is one definition of a miracle.

Thanking heaven even for our difficulties and misfortunes is the best way to transform them. You will see your difficulties in a different light, as if you had wrapped them in a film of pure gold.

OMRAAM MIKHAEL AIVANHOV

When I look back, there have been many long weeks when the only human contact I'd have was with the check-out clerk at the grocery store. I shunned everyone. I didn't go to my other Twelve Step meetings because I resented everyone for their healthy bodies. I stayed home and felt sorry for myself.

When I did socialize, I was often cranky and let everyone know about how miserable I was. I mostly stayed home and overate and zoned out, watching TV and playing on the computer. I was caught in a downward cycle. I planned my suicide. I resented all the people who didn't call, who had abandoned me.

It was a time in my life when I was sure that nothing good would ever happen to me, that my condition would get worse, that I'd lost everything that was important to me, and that I would be stuck living out the rest of my days angry, depressed, in pain, and alone.

I look back now and am grateful for discovering CPA. My life and attitude are totally transformed today. How did it happen? I can't exactly say. I believe the Steps are the solution, and that I had been living in the problem.

Going to CPA meetings and working through the Twelve Steps changed my life. It made it possible for me to connect with my Higher Power and learn new ways to think, to act, to live. The Steps are the essence of the program and opened up a beautiful new world, after I thought mine was over.

Gratitude is the intention to count your blessings every day, every minute, while avoiding, whenever possible, the belief that you need or deserve different circumstances.

TIMOTHY MILLER

Years ago, I put great emphasis on perfection for the holidays. As the Mom, I believed it was my job to cook the big meal for everyone and make it a splendid feast. This meant days of shopping, cooking, and cleaning, which would put me over the edge, and I'd pay for it physically and emotionally for weeks afterwards. Little by little, I let go of my insanity. We'd go to a restaurant, had a potluck one year, and once we went to the house of another family member. I learned to let go of tradition and open to God's guidance as to how the holidays would be celebrated each year.

There have been years I was totally alone and wept my way through the holidays. There were times I resented all the family being here; years I resented that the kids went to be with their dad. The fact is, I was never happy, no matter what happened.

Finally, I let go and let God.

I've learned to see life as perfect under any circumstances. Being alone can be a gift. It is my attitude of acceptance and ability to take care of my own needs that determines the quality of my celebration, not the circumstances. This year my adult children will not be home, and I will be alone for Thanksgiving. Yes, I am invited to various places, but I don't want to go. I am taking care of myself by not pushing myself to socialize. I am thrilled! If you had told me years ago that would be my reaction, I'd think you were nuts.

The more I turn my life and will over to the care of God, the more I can be present and joyful about whatever shows up. This comes from the power of working the Steps in CPA. I can let go of all the "shoulds" of how a holiday is supposed to look, and be in gratitude for how it does look—gratitude for the freedom to make my own choices, for having a roof over my head and money to buy food, for being loved and having a loving family and friends, whether I am with them or not.

Become a possibilitarian. No matter how dark things seem to be or actually are, raise your sights and see possibilities—always see them, for they're always there.

NORMAN VINCENT PEALE

When I was able to walk, I loved the beach. Now that I'm confined to a wheelchair… not so much. It is a constant reminder of what used to be and what is not now present in my life.

When we were planning a family vacation, my son and wife both jumped on "The Beach!" I didn't say much. As the time approached, in my mind I was plotting how to get out of this trip. How would I deal with the wheelchair and my constant pain at the beach? It would only increase my difficulty.

Then, in a moment of total clarity, I realized that my only child was going away to college in two weeks. The person who had been at the center of my life for the past eighteen years was leaving. This trip to the beach had nothing to do with me, and everything to do with family. I went back to my training in the program, of living one moment at a time, and not looking at the whole trip.

Now, I'm having an outstanding time with my family at the beach! We found a place close to the boardwalk so I can have something to entertain me and still be close to my family. They play on the beach in the morning, and we meet for lunch in the village downtown. I wheel about town with ease in my wheelchair. We find family things to do in the afternoons. Yesterday we went down to a great little crab restaurant for dinner, then off to see the wild horses that live on a nearby island. The travel gods were with us—we got close to some of the horses in our car as they were feeding at dusk.

Once again I learned that, "One Day at a Time," I can do darn near anything.

In the darkest hour the soul is replenished and given strength to continue and endure.

Heart Warrior Chosa

A tumor growing inside my spinal cord came back, and I had more surgery, which left me a paraplegic with neuropathic pain. Some time later, I met with my neurosurgeon and was told the tumor had returned, yet again. The unexpected news was not welcome. I immediately said the Serenity Prayer over and over in my mind.

When I left the doctor's office, I sat in my van, alone with my thoughts. Usually over-thinking makes things worse. This time, my program led me to create a mental gratitude list, looking at how far I've come since the first surgery.

I've worked hard and accepted being a paraplegic. I learned how to drive again and can move around on my own. I've come to terms with living with a wheelchair and made changes so my home is accessible. I've made peace with my pain. I have a loving, supportive family.

A few days later, a dear friend sent me a note that brought everything into perspective. My friend wrote: "I don't like it when God gives us these opportunities to work our program. They aren't fun or easy, even though, often down the road, we are grateful. There are so many emotions and decisions to navigate through, and we struggle with our loss of equilibrium as our world shifts yet again."

These words remind me that life is not about the goal but about the journey. We have no control of the cards life has dealt us; what counts is how we play the hand.

When seen as a rite of initiation rather than as a disfiguring or disabling force, every illness becomes a path to a particular healing or personal gift. If we listen deeply to its message rather than try to eliminate it, illness may heal us instead of the other way around.

ESTELLE FRANKEL

After surgery I found myself having to learn to walk again. Much to my dismay I required a cane to keep from falling down. This was a big adjustment, but I was coping. Then, as the pain grew and my functionality decreased, I found myself in a destructive downward spiral of depression, low self-esteem, uncontrolled weight gain, and growing isolation from my friends and family. I looked at what my life had become and believed no one in the world had ever faced the losses I was experiencing. I felt very alone.

To help with the pain, my doctors were prescribing medications that were dulling my mind and making it impossible to carry on lengthy conversations. I kept forgetting what I wanted to say. Although reading is something that has sustained me all my life, the medications affected my ability to concentrate, so I could no longer read. I kept having to give up valued pieces of my life.

I was in a hopeless state of mind. That was when I discovered that using the Twelve Steps of CPA got me in touch with my emotional pain. I did the intense work of re-examining my life from the perspective of how I was letting chronic pain and illness dictate it. Going through the Steps with my sponsor and changing my attitude saved my life, my family, and my ability to function. I thank God for that every day.

Everything can be taken from a man but one thing; the last of human freedoms—to choose one's attitude in any given set of circumstances, to choose one's own way.

VIKTOR FRANKL

I was out-of-town to share in a family celebration and had come home in bad shape. It is hard enough when my body is in pain, but even more challenging is my mental state. When my body is so low functioning, my mind has a tendency to move into negative gear. All those damaging thoughts I was sure I was done with, come rushing in "...life isn't worth living, I can't do anything, so clearly I'm a total loser, poor pitiful me." These dark thoughts blot out any possibility of hope or gratitude. I don't want to consider gratitude. I'm miserable and I just want to stay that way. It takes too much energy to even think, let alone reach for sunny gratitude when all I see is dark clouds.

This, too, shall pass. And, it's true. I can remember being in this low place before, and I know that I always move out of it once my pain subsides and my energy stores are recharged. This is not my forever. It is my "Just for Today."

When I am this ill, the world shrinks my vision into a narrow view, and all I see is me and my suffering. I can't see beyond my own pain. I might even hang on tight to it. But then I remember to "Let Go and Let God." I remember to open my mind and let go of the tight grasp I have on my pain and my limited perspective of the world.

Just opening the door a bit to gratitude, and writing out my feelings and thoughts, brings in fresh air. I am grateful to be willing. I am grateful to know I don't have to stay stuck in my old thinking. I am grateful to all the program friends who listen and don't judge. Soon enough, gratitude expands my vision, and I find hope one more time.

The habit of being happy enables one to be freed, or largely freed, from domination of outside conditions.

ROBERT LOUIS STEVENSON

This morning, after many days of pain and sleepless nights, I was lying in bed dreading the day ahead, when I had a God moment, and realized that I had a choice. It was not inevitable that I had to be a grouchy, irritable person who was angry at her body and everyone who dared come near. I had a choice as to how I would think and feel about myself, my day, and those I encounter.

I have always believed I am stuck being darkly negative until the pain subsides and regular sleep returns, that my level of positivity depends on outside forces, such as improvement in my health. Wrong. That thinking was my character defect. Today, God removed it and showed me a different way. My attitude changed, and that is another step in my recovery journey.

Today I chose to go through my day loving my body and my life, and did my best to have a smile on my face. Will I be able to do it tomorrow? I don't know. I am grateful for this one moment of clarity, of awareness that my attitude and thinking is what will create the kind of day I am going to have, not my bodily state or amount of sleep. With my experiment in choosing a positive attitude, my day was wonderful and all was well.

If for a moment we make way with our petty selves, wish no ill to anything, apprehend no ill, cease to be but a crystal which reflects a ray,—what shall we not reflect! What a universe will appear crystallized and radiant around us!

HENRY DAVID THOREAU

I have an "invisible" illness with only scarce medical research indicating it is real. When I first became ill, not only did nobody rally around me, they were insulting and questioned my mental health. It felt like no one understood and that friends and family abandoned me. I felt disregarded and ignored.

A year later, when a friend developed breast cancer, she got lots of attention. People were supportive of her by coming to her house with meals and helping her through surgery, chemotherapy, and recovery. I was jealous of her!

My self-importance was greatly distorted. I was angry about my situation. I was sure that I had it worse than my friend, as my illness couldn't be cut out or cured. Didn't I need even *more* attention than her?

I definitely needed a Power greater than myself to restore me to sanity. The CPA program of recovery helped me become humble and see my place in the world. I learned that I am not the center of the universe, even when I am sick and in pain and believe I deserve to be the center. Through working the Steps, talking with my sponsor, and praying for my character defects to be removed, little by little, my attitude has changed. I have new tools for coping when feelings like anger and jealousy appear.

I am powerless over people, places, and things, but I can ask for what I need when I am struggling. It doesn't mean I will always get a yes response, but when things don't work out as I had planned I trust that my Higher Power has another, better plan for me to follow.

Sanity has even come from doing service work. Now, when a friend becomes ill, I have compassion instead of envy. Through my words and actions I can pass along the strength and courage I've received in CPA. There is value in my experience, and now I have something that I can give, rather than demand to receive.

I have found that if you love life, life will love you back.

ARTHUR RUBENSTEIN

I have always been a person with a positive attitude in life, the guy who sees the glass as half full. It has served me well over the years, and especially now.

For people with chronic pain and illness it can be difficult to go out into the world with a happy face. The pain tends to drag down the corners of our lips like a heavy weight. It can be harder for us to embark on our day than it is for many other people—even to get out of bed, or to drink the first cup of coffee, or to get into the shower. We sometimes need help to get dressed or to put on our shoes. Sometimes we are unable to hold down a job, or our hours of work have to be shortened to allow time to replenish our energy.

Despite these difficulties, I embark on each day with a happy face, and also make a point of engaging people in the course of my daily life. I am a human who needs other people. I need to engage in conversation, if only for 30 seconds—the grocery store clerk, the gas station attendant, the people at the dry cleaners.

My interaction with others goes much better if I'm positive and honest. This program allows me to be this way. I work the Steps every day in order to go out as an authentic me, not one that needs to prop himself up to put on a positive act. Even if I am having a bad pain day, positive interactions with people are tonic for what ails me.

FELLOWSHIP

Kind words can be short and easy to speak, but their echoes are truly endless.

MOTHER TERESA

After I became ill I began losing friends. I tried to stay in touch, but one by one, they disappeared. There were the people who stopped calling to invite me to social activities because I had cancelled at the last minute one time too many. There were people whose calls got fewer and far between because each time they phoned all they heard were the stories of the latest procedure that didn't work or the latest drug with side effects. There were the people I worked with, but once we no longer had that in common, we found we had very little in common.

I mourned the loss of these friends and acquaintances. For a time I felt very alone and isolated. But the ending of these connections opened the door to a new and wonderful world. When I came to CPA I discovered people who understood me. I didn't have to explain why I didn't get out of bed until 1:00 PM and didn't have the energy to brush my teeth. I didn't have to explain why I could only talk for 5 minutes on the telephone. They understand when I talk about feelings of anger and disappointment. They don't try to fix me. They just listen and care.

My best friend now lives 3,000 miles away, but she is just an email or a phone call away. I can count on my new friends to be compassionate when I call them in tears. They don't judge me or try to tell me what I need to do. In this new life I've learned to laugh again. I've learned that together we can get through anything. I may have to live with pain and illness, but I don't have to do it alone. Yes, some old friends were lost, but today, there are new loving friends who help me along a spiritual path that brings healing.

If you want to go quickly, go alone. If you want to go far, go together.

A**FRICAN** **PROVERB**

I remember coming home from school as a child, and my mother would be crying but would never talk about it. I thought it was my fault, and began to believe that *everything* was my fault. This became a life-long pattern.

Recently I was with a CPA friend who has been in recovery for a couple of years, and she strongly suggested I find a sponsor. She said it was important to work the Twelve Steps with another person, that I can't do them by myself. It's hard for me to let another person get to know me. It makes me feel too vulnerable when someone sees me at my worst, in pain or crying. I don't want to share all my faults and experience the shame that results from being so exposed. I'm afraid my vulnerability will push others away.

At meetings I've heard others talk about turning problems over to a Higher Power. It sounds wonderful not to be alone and get help. I'd like to turn my fear of sharing my feelings over to a Higher Power, but I don't know if I believe in one. I want to discover whether I have a Higher Power, too. This is why I need a sponsor. I want to learn to trust.

The place to start is to reach out and ask someone to be my sponsor.

Though we travel the world over to find the beautiful, we must carry it with us or we find it not.

RALPH WALDO EMERSON

Generally when I was vulnerable, it triggered feelings of shame, and all I wanted to do was hide under a blanket and not be seen. The last thing I wanted was to become exposed, with my raw, unprotected emotions and thoughts flapping in the wind. To be able to share my vulnerability with another person is an act of bravery, so I am grateful to all those who have taken the risk by sharing in meetings and taught me it is OK to be myself.

Now when I go to a meeting I can open myself to many people at once, and listen as well. I once heard someone at a meeting say, "God does not create junk," and realized that when I feel vulnerable it is sometimes because I am telling myself I am junk. My mind is playing tricks on me with stories of self-pity and of futures filled with tragic endings that a "bad" person like me deserves. I don't have to do this to myself anymore.

Remembering that my Higher Power created me, and in His eyes I am perfect, opens me to accepting myself just as I am in the moment, even when I feel like this body has betrayed me and wish I could trade it in for a newer model. When I see myself through the eyes of my Higher Power—as expressed by my friends in the program and a loving sponsor—I begin to have hope again and am willing to receive the blessings my Higher Power offers.

My current sponsor is someone I can trust with anything, and she will listen with kindness. Sometimes she will gently help me get out of the hole I've dug, or guide me in a more effective direction. She does not judge me, and the result is that over time I judge myself less. This is a slow journey of recovery, and, thanks to CPA, the healing of my mind and spirit continue as the result of our gentle, caring fellowship.

The most beautiful people we have known are those who have known defeat, known suffering, known struggle, known loss, and have found their way out of the depths. These persons have an appreciation, a sensitivity and an understanding of life that fills them with compassion, gentleness, and a deep loving concern.

ELISABETH KÜBLER-ROSS

Step Two gives us hope, showing us there is a way out—if we are willing to let go of our need to control our chronic condition and to accept that there are spiritual resources available. We don't have to struggle with pain and illness alone.

A basic element of how to find recovery in CPA is to let go of our need to control our body and accept help from our Higher Power. Doing this is liberating.

The tricky part is that when pain and illness are most acute is precisely the hardest time for us to try out a new behavior and attitude. We just want to be relieved of our misery. It is hard to remember that our Higher Power is there for us.

I heard someone in a meeting say that they go to meetings and work on their program even when their life is calm, because they can store up the benefits, like money in the bank. Then when life throws that curve ball, the resources are there. I find that it is important to work on my attitude and ability to "Let Go and Let God" with the small things, so that I build up enough skill and strength for when the difficult times appear.

The Twelve Step slogans and tools are little lifesavers that pop up at just the right moment to get me through an hour, through a day. God sends me angels, people who say the right thing, who touch me in a loving way, who help me see hope when all is dark. During one very bad night I totally got lost. I was ready to throw out the program altogether. But one small part of me knew what to do, so I picked up the phone and called a program friend. My dear friend reminded me that I was strong and that I would get through my difficulties. I had lost my faith, my hope, and my connection to God that evening. But God had not lost me.

One of the most calming and powerful actions you can do to intervene in a stormy world is to stand up and show your soul. Struggling souls catch light from other souls who are fully lit and willing to show it.

CLARISSA PINKOLA ESTES

When I first came to CPA I didn't quite understand why anonymity was such a big deal. It is no secret that I live with pain and illness. It doesn't matter to me who knows my name or that I am ill, as there is nothing to hide. My cane is a dead giveaway.

Now that I've been around for a while, I understand there is more to anonymity than just protecting my privacy. When I attend a meeting, there are people from all walks of life. Some receive food stamps, are unable to work, and struggle financially. Some people have disability insurance and so have a steady income, even if it is less than they had in the past. Some have a partner who works and they live quite comfortably. There are those with doctorate degrees and people who never graduated from high school. Many come from other Twelve Step programs, and many others don't. Anonymity is about leaving my social status, bank account, and other programs outside the CPA meetings. I come as a fellow sufferer of chronic pain and chronic illness.

I also leave my specific condition outside the meeting rooms. By doing this we become inclusive to everyone. No one is "terminally unique." I am not defined by my condition. In this way, everyone feels welcome. All that is needed to be a member of CPA is to live with chronic pain or chronic illness.

Through anonymity we are not distracted by the "bondage of self" and are open to being teachable through the program. It doesn't matter if I have cancer and you have a back injury from an accident. It matters that we both suffer from the emotional effects of physical dis-ease, and we can help each other by living the Twelve Steps of CPA.

In the depth of winter, I finally learned that within me there lay an invincible summer.

ALBERT CAMUS

It feels as though chronic pain has stripped me down and exposed every vulnerability I ever had...and as a result I've found a whole new way to live. Pain has humbled me, and today I'm grateful for it. Yes, grateful for the pain, and all I learn from it!

It's a process, starting with the First Step. I was powerless over the pain, which resulted in feelings like depression, anger, fear, jealousy, isolation, self-pity, shame, anxiety, resentment, and on and on. When I admitted to myself that the feelings were a result of living with chronic pain, I was then able to begin to change the way I reacted.

Again, it's a process and not a one-time event. I need to practice the Steps and be willing to do the work. I need willingness to do things differently and courage to sustain my desire to grow. Some days I fall back into old thoughts and behaviors and need to start again. But each day, and each moment with pain, gives me another chance to put the principles of recovery to work. Practice, practice, practice!

I try not to worry about tomorrow, because that's when the fear starts to kick in. Then I pick up the phone and call my sponsor or someone else in CPA, and read the CPA literature. All these things become second nature and automatic. I give it time, and, most importantly, keep coming back to CPA to be reminded how to live without suffering, and to maintain a sense of hope and courage. I gain tremendous strength to carry on. We all have our struggles, but when we come together to love and support one another, eventually miracles truly do happen.

If I have been of service, if I have glimpsed more of the nature and essence of ultimate good, if I am inspired to reach wider horizons of thought and action, if I am at peace with myself, it has been a successful day.

ALEX NOBLE

What is CPA service doing for me? It has given me a sense of purpose and a sense of fellowship.

I have lived with chronic pain of some sort for over thirty years, and it has taken its toll. Before I found CPA, my self-esteem had plummeted. I felt like I had nothing to give, and that I would never be of use to anyone, ever again. I used to be good at my job, caring for my home, and enjoyed several hobbies, but due to pain I was no longer able to engage in those activities, so I felt useless. Anything I could still do, I felt was done inadequately.

After a few months in CPA I became involved with service. At first I felt I didn't have much to give, but after being involved for a time this changed, and what I gave came back tenfold.

For the most part, I have discovered a lessening of my pain when working with a sponsee or another member of CPA. I, too, was concerned about not being able to give, or run a meeting, or accept responsibility for a particular role in CPA. What I have discovered about doing service is there's an understanding that on any given day I may not be up to the task for which I am responsible. When that happens, and I have to ask for help, it is provided without question. People in this fellowship understand, like nowhere else, that some days just suck, and I can't do it, whatever "it" is. This also made it easier to ask for help, something I haven't done well in the past.

In CPA we understand one another on the physical and the emotional level, which, in my book, is true understanding. And we all give, to ourselves and to each other. I never would have known the joy and the fellowship of recovery if I hadn't stepped forward and offered whatever I could give. And though it may sound unselfish, in truth, it is my selfishness that brought me to participate in service, because I need it for my self-worth and my recovery. As they say, "We have to give it away to keep it."

Let no one ever come to you without leaving better and happier. Be the living expression of God's kindness: kindness in your face, kindness in your eyes, kindness in your smile.

MOTHER TERESA

When first reading the Steps I thought I'd never reach Step Twelve. It seemed I didn't need to worry about doing any service work until I got there. But then I realized that service begins as soon as we make the decision to do something about our unmanageable lives.

When I started to learn about the Twelve Steps and what recovery meant, I automatically had begun to do service. When I decided to give CPA a chance, I was doing myself a great service. From then on, it was a process of continuing to learn what true service meant to myself, my Higher Power, and finally, to the CPA fellowship.

Doing service or carrying the message can be as simple as sharing at a meeting or posting on an online meeting. There seem to be endless opportunities to help the next person who is hurting or struggling. Just sharing what a terrible day we had can draw others out of their own awful day, because they do not feel so alone with their problems. If that happens, we've done a service. There are times when just hearing about how someone else used program tools to get through a terrible day can make a person a little less willing to give in to despair. Or better yet, they themselves reach out to help someone else.

When I am able to help another who is struggling, my struggles are somehow eased. My pain is less severe, and I feel better about myself. Doing service, or *"carrying the message to others living with chronic pain and chronic illness,"* can be as simple as picking up the phone or e-mailing a message. It doesn't always take much effort to make a difference.

In everyone's life, at some time, our inner fire goes out. It is then burst into flame by an encounter with another human being. We should all be thankful for those people who rekindle the inner spirit.

ALBERT SCHWEITZER

Isolate means, "set apart or cut off from others." It comes from a root word that means "made into an island." By nature, I am independent, so it is not natural for me to reach out to others when I am in trouble. Doing my Steps helped me see the ways I chose to keep myself cut off, and to realize that asking for help is a way to make amends to myself. I am still always learning how to do this.

Most of us spent years living as healthy persons, so when we became ill, we entered a new culture. It was as if all the rules of living no longer applied. We still live among the same people as before, but we no longer know how to relate to ourselves, let alone our friends and family. For many, the tendency is to shut down, crawl into our cave, and lick our wounds. We feel very alone, physically and emotionally, and very much like an island that no one really understands.

The antidote is involvement with others. CPA gives us lots of ways to achieve this. First, just attending a meeting, sharing, doing service work and reaching out to others gets us out of our own small space and expands our world. We find that we are not alone in what we experience, feel, and think. For me, this was such a healing discovery. The fellowship of CPA meant that I was no longer an island, or at the very least, I was part of a chain of islands.

CPA gave me many tools to shift my attitude. Then I found willingness to let go of isolation and gently walk through the fears, shame, and self-pity that kept me from reaching out. One example is acting "as if," which helps me behave differently, even though it might feel awkward at first. And with each small success, I am lifted more and more out of my isolation.

FREEDOM FROM THE BONDAGE OF SELF

We are each of us angels with only one wing, and we can only fly by embracing one another.

LUCIANO DE CRESCENZO

I grew up in an abusive family and as a result learned how to protect myself by becoming self-sufficient, strong, and competent. When I became ill I could no longer be any of these and did not know how to cope with the changes. I began to isolate.

Being with others was difficult. The effects of my illness made me so tired it was difficult to care about socializing, and the effects of my medications impaired my ability to function. I alternated between going into too much detail about my illness and pain, to hiding out and not answering the phone.

Little by little, with my recent recognition of my powerlessness, and asking for help from my Higher Power, I've come to realize that I need other people. This still scares me. However, I have been asking for help in order to shed the armor I've worn all my life. I want to be open to others and feel close to them. I want to accept the gifts of friendship and love.

I am tentatively living in a new way, experiencing miracles that I don't quite yet trust. I used to believe there was no future after becoming ill. Today, my mind is open and I am willing to learn new ways of relating, to myself and others.

Knowing others is intelligence; knowing yourself is true wisdom.
Mastering others is strength; mastering yourself is true power.

Tao Te Ching

Over the years I have become very self-centered and self-involved. My chronic pain and illness has affected my family and those around me. I have to a great extent been the focus of the family.

My partner has recently been diagnosed with a serious health issue and is now facing a future of chronic pain. While I have immense compassion in my heart for her, there is a part of me that is jealous, because now I have to share the spotlight.

Today, however, because of working the Steps, I can see my self-centeredness and move beyond it, recognizing this part of me, and doing the right thing anyway. Because of recovery, I can identify "my stuff," see it for what it is, and move on. I don't have to let my selfishness and jealousy get in the way anymore. I have a choice, as my sponsor has told me.

Further, I need to be there for my partner; and because of the Steps and my Higher Power, I can do that. I'm learning to take care of myself today, and because of that I can be there for someone else, in spite of any pain or jealousy I still might feel. When I am helping someone else, especially someone with chronic pain and illness, I no longer feel as jealous, or self-centered, or sorry for myself. Those feelings tend to leave when I am being of service to others. And at times, the pain lessens or even disappears.

So today, while recognizing that there is room for growth, I'm not so hard on myself. I know I am heading in the right direction.

I am not discouraged, because every wrong attempt discarded is another step forward.

THOMAS A. EDISON

Many areas of our lives change with the onset of chronic illness and pain, and one of those areas is physical intimacy. One of the losses in this area is spontaneity. In the past I took for granted the sweetness of having these connections just happen. I did not realize the value of that until it was no longer a part of the rhythm of my days and nights.

My husband and I have had to become accustomed to adjusting this area of our life around my physical condition and my level of pain. Because sleep is so crucial to my well-being, and I no longer sleep without taking sleep aids, my sleep time is regimented and scheduled. I have a set time when I begin to take medications in order to be able to go sleep. If I do begin to fall asleep, but the process is interrupted, I often can't get back to sleep for hours. If I don't get a good night's sleep, the next day the pain is multiplied, so it has become of paramount importance to get a good night's sleep. As a result of my pain, we lost our previous, natural time for physical intimacy. We have learned to "schedule" intimacy in, but it has not been easy. There has been resentment on both sides. He is disappointed at the loss of the spontaneity and having to make this fit into a schedule, rather than happening naturally like it did in the past. My resentment appears when I suffer the physical consequences of saying yes to his desire when it does not fit my plan for pain management.

We love each other and want to be respectful of each other's needs, so we make the effort to do the best we can with what we have. We both sometimes sacrifice what we want for the good of the other and our relationship. The Twelve Step program of CPA has taught me that I have no control over the fact that I have a chronic illness, and this has helped me to accept what is. I have learned to make adjustments and take care of myself, while sometimes also making a choice outside my regimen. My husband and I have worked together to keep this important part of our lives fun and meaningful. It is the new normal, and continues to enrich our relationship. It is progress, not perfection.

Our listening creates a sanctuary for the homeless parts within the other person.

RACHEL NAOMI REMEN

When I am caught up in isolation and loneliness and chronic pain, I think that the only way I can get better emotionally is to have someone reach out and care for me. Until now, I didn't realize that by getting outside of myself and helping others that I, in fact, will be helped. It truly is by changing my thinking 180 degrees that my world has taken on a whole different perspective.

Through listening to and learning from others in the fellowship, I am beginning to understand how this attitude change works in my life. Now I need to practice the change, little by little, each day. When I start to feel lonely, I pick up the telephone and reach out to others.

Today I called my Great Aunt, who lives alone and also lives with chronic pain. She was so happy to hear from me. We both made ourselves a cup of tea, and it felt like she was right there in the living room with me. We laughed about old times. By the time we hung up, I was no longer feeling sad and isolated.

It is one of the most beautiful compensations of this life that no man can sincerely try to help another without also helping himself.

RALPH WALDO EMERSON

I've noticed how my state of mind can affect the level of my pain. When I obsess and focus only on myself and the pain, I notice my pain level increases. But when I choose a loving, compassionate attitude it helps me to relax, and the pain eases. Understanding this has been a gift of practicing the Twelve Step program of CPA.

I was working at a home-based daycare, and several of the babies had been very fussy, so I decided to spend some extra time snuggling with each one. As I did this, giving them my unconditional love, I was blessed to receive their love in return.

The week ended on Valentine's Day. That morning, one of the babies arrived terribly constipated. I've never seen a human being struggle so painfully. She screamed and cried, pushing hard while balling up her tiny little fists, turning red and even sweating as she struggled. All I could do to comfort her was hold her, console her, and love her. I wanted nothing more than to help her get through *her* pain. And it was then that I realized I was completely unaware of my own. I felt such a deep love and compassion for this little girl as I cried along with her, and as a result, my own pain became insignificant.

This very personal experience has shown me what a powerful role the heart and mind can play in the level of my pain and my perception of it. I guess it could be a coincidence that this experience occurred on Valentine's Day, but I don't see it that way. This was a spiritual experience for me, without a doubt. But just in case I needed a hint, my Higher Power sent a very clear one. It came in the form of the child's name. Her name was Grace.

ONE DAY AT A TIME

It is a mistake to look too far ahead. Only one link in the chain of destiny can be handled at a time.

Sir Winston Churchill

I can get into trouble when I start thinking about my life down the road. I have a tendency to imagine the worst, and get caught up in writing tragic movies in my head. Then I start reacting with sadness and anger to this horrible future as though it had actually happened, even though it exists only in my head.

The slogan, "Just for Today," snaps me back into reality. It reminds me that all I have to do is the "next indicated action." I don't have to figure out my entire life this afternoon. I do have to figure out what to eat for dinner and finish a load of laundry, but these are quite manageable.

It's a waste of time thinking too much about the future, because the future is filled with surprises. When I think back to times of crisis, I remember that they did not last forever, even though I was sure at the time they would. I was always able to rise to the challenges that showed up.

Lately I have developed new diseases, with new pains associated with them. These are problems that are progressive and will increase debilitation, so it does scare me when I get caught in future thinking. Thankfully, CPA gives me tools to move through my thoughts and emotions in ways that serve me and improve the quality of my life. These tools lift me out of my old thinking and empower me to move forward with hope and joy.

CPA reminds me that all I have to do is focus on the next 12 hours, 6 hours, 1 hour, 1 minute. I know I can manage this. And the rest I can turn over to my Higher Power who has provided for me wonderfully: a referral to a great doctor, a friend to call when I am scared and confused, a refund in the mail to cover the cost of repairing the car. New drugs and treatments are always coming on the market. The future is yet to be determined.

So when I find myself going down that road of "I can't bear the thought of living like this for the rest of my life," I grab onto this tool and shift my attention to what is in front of me. Yes, I can do anything for twelve hours. When I remember this, my courage and resourcefulness, along with my faith in my Higher Power, returns, and I choose to embrace another day.

Live in the present. Do the things that need to be done. Do all the good you can each day. The future will unfold.

PEACE PILGRIM

Someone once said something about "God's pile and my pile." Since at the time I was a single mom with six kids, the first piles I thought of were laundry piles! I got this great picture in my head of two big piles of dirty laundry. My job is to wash, dry, and fold my own pile, and leave God's alone. And I don't get to push Him if I think I'm finished before He is. He has a different timetable, and that is none of my business.

In Step Seven, *"Humbly asked Him to remove our shortcomings,"* the piles consist of my defects. I get to do as much humble footwork on them as possible. Sometimes the stains come right out, other times they don't. But I do my best, over and over again. (There's *always* another pile of dirty laundry!) It's God's job to get the really tough stains out, and sometimes that takes a while. Several washings, in fact.

It's pretty clear to me that the fact that I have pain, and that it seems to get worse each year, belongs in God's pile. That awareness is easy, and acceptance follows quickly. A bit more difficult is becoming aware of which activities can cause my pain to increase, and then making the choice to go ahead with my plans and accept the increased pain, or simply accept that this is something I can no longer do. Life is so much easier once I gain the awareness of what I can leave in God's pile.

And of course, I'm always reminded that I'm going to wear those clothes again, and will probably find myself with a big chocolate stain of arrogance on one again ... or the blueberry stains of impatience.

Neither I, nor my clothes, will ever be perfect, but God doesn't like a mess either, so I know He'll keep working on His pile. I just need to keep up with mine. It's all a very humbling and wonderfully gentle process.

To live is to wrestle with despair, yet never to allow despair to have the last word.

CORNEL WEST

I noticed recently that it is much easier to use the program when my pain is minimal, and much more difficult when I am feeling extreme pain or illness. A couple of days ago I was hit unexpectedly with a severe relapse of my chronic condition. Day One, I was down most of the day and feeling pretty depressed and discouraged. I knew I should try to look for help in CPA but was just too far down to do anything. I let myself grieve and feel it. Day Two hit and I was still feeling awful and unable to do much. I struggled to think of things to help me deal with it. I planned to call my sponsor but did not get around to it.

Even in this withdrawn, angry, and grieving state, I was able to reach for my CPA tools and get the help I needed. I thought of the gratitude list and forced myself to do some of that. I kept reminding myself that this, too, shall pass. Just because I feel rotten now doesn't mean that I will feel rotten always. I had felt quite well for a few months so I was not prepared when this decline hit. I turned it over to my Higher Power a few times, telling Him that I trust Him with my life. I read through my CPA slogans and journal and found encouragement. These tools have helped me make it through. They alleviated some of my emotional pain and depression, but it was still rough.

This is Day Three, and I'm really hoping that tomorrow I wake up feeling better, but then remind myself to live just for today. Reading the *One Day at a Time* bookmark is helping me today. It is filled with good thoughts for times like these: living each day to best of my ability, whatever my ability is for that day, and not dwelling on the negative; remembering that I am more than my pain or illness and accepting whatever comes my way with an attitude of gratitude; accepting the conditions of my life as they are this day; acknowledging feelings of fear and anxiety as they rise up and remembering to put my trust in my Higher Power; knowing that I can live, and even thrive, through anything, when I do it one moment at a time.

SELF-CARE

Consider the little mouse, how sagacious an animal it is which never entrusts his life to one hole only.

PLAUTUS

I find that sometimes I create powerless situations for myself. Because of my all-or-nothing thinking I decide that if I can't participate in an activity or event in the exact way I planned ahead of time, then I can't be involved at all.

For example, I had a big family celebration coming up, and I was afraid my pain would flare and I wouldn't be able to participate. Extended family was coming from out-of-town, and I was hosting the weekend at my house. I was afraid I'd ruin the weekend for everyone. My sponsor suggested using the tool of having a back-up plan.

Plan A was preparing for the weekend by maintaining good self-care routines consistently, for at least the week before they arrived. It also included planning ahead and moderating the amount of prep work I did each day. It was setting myself up for success and assuming I could engage fully in the weekend.

Plan B was doing all the prep work of Plan A, but with a back-up plan of building in a daily rest time in the afternoon if the pain started to become unmanageable. I would still be involved in morning and evening activities.

Plan C was doing all the prep work of Plan A, using the back-up plan of Plan B, and eating all meals out if my pain reached severe levels. I would delegate as many tasks as possible. My goal would be to *be* with people instead of *doing* for people. I would let go of my expectations of the perfect weekend. I would rejoice in the relationships I could still fully enjoy, instead of feeling defeated by the tasks I could not fully engage in.

Today I have choices, and I make them, so that my pain no longer completely determines what I can do and enjoy.

We have the power to direct our minds to replace the feelings of being upset, depressed, and fearful with the feeling of inner peace.

GERALD G. JAMPOLSKY

I try to meditate most days, and it can be different each time. Sometimes my mind slows down and there is an expansive feeling of spaciousness. Other times it is an intense spiritual experience, which opens my heart and mind. When I have these feelings, it becomes easy and natural to hand myself over to the care of my Higher Power.

When meditating, I feel closest to my Higher Power. During these times, I can sense a part of myself as an observer. This observer has a great capacity for peacefulness in the face of whatever is happening in my life. I seem to merge into a universal loving feeling, and staying in that place does me a world of good. There, some of the self-critical thoughts and self-dislike that may hang around me can just dissolve away into this lovingness.

Through these experiences of a loving Higher Power, I am beginning to feel separated from the painful messages from my childhood. I see the possibility of experiencing happiness, joy, and freedom, even with the challenges I face.

The only way out is through. The only way to heal the pain is to embrace the pain.

FRITZ PERLS

Acceptance can be a difficult principle when it comes to living with chronic pain. It has taken a long time for me to realize that acceptance is not about giving up or giving in. I have come to understand that simple acceptance of reality is the opposite of denial.

When I tried to run from the chronic pain, I found it didn't go away; in fact, I noticed how drained and hopeless I felt. When I finally decided to accept that chronic pain was a reality, just for today, I could direct my energy toward positive ways of working with it.

Today I choose to cope with pain without blaming God, myself, or anyone else. I do my best to keep my fear and my anger in check. I want to live today in healthier ways than I have in the past.

Acceptance helps me realize that each day brings new opportunities for me to discover ways to work with the pain in a positive way. I may do this by asking my body what it needs today. Do I need rest, a healthy meal, quiet time in prayer and meditation? Or do I need to talk with a friend or take the dog for a walk outside in the fresh air?

I can stop struggling to want what used to be and instead find the "good" in today. I also know that each day is another day in which medical science might find a better way to treat me. But even if this doesn't happen, I find acceptance helps me to live in a way that conserves my resources and adds to my peace and joy, "One Day at a Time."

Knowing when to say no and when to say yes is the beginning of true wisdom.

RALPH T. RUPERT

Last weekend my daughter asked me to babysit for my grand-children. I love my grandchildren, and it gives me great pleasure to spend time with them. But my daughter and her husband weren't going to return home until late, and I knew that I needed to stick to my self-care routine to maintain my current level of functioning. With much guilt and regret, I told my daughter I would not be able to care for the children.

Why is it that I don't want to disappoint others? Why am I willing to jeopardize my health and well-being and agree to do something I know is not in my best interest? When I make a choice to take care of myself by saying "no" to someone else, it is true the other person may feel annoyed or even angry. But more often than not, their reaction is temporary. It passes. When I don't tend to my own needs, I disappoint myself and sometimes end up struggling with pain and other symptoms, for days. It's also true that the other party may *not* get angry, but instead express gratitude at my open and honest sharing. Either way, it is their decision, not mine.

A year ago I would not have been able to say "no" to my daughter even though it meant risking my own well-being, but today I was able to make a different choice. I struggled with guilt because I may have disappointed her, but at least I was able to see that I had an option and acted on it. This is progress, not perfection. Today I know the benefits of saying "no" to others and "yes" to self-care.

… all shall be well, and all shall be well, and all manner of thing shall be well.

JULIAN OF NORWICH

Resting *is* doing something. Resting is *not* doing nothing. It may sound a bit strange but let me explain. When I was first in CPA I found it difficult to embrace the concept of taking care of myself if it meant not getting things done. I have always been a dependable person and am accustomed to keeping up with my responsibilities. This trait of reliability became compromised when my customary good health gave way to chronic illness and pain.

At first I struggled to keep up with everything, but the result was more pain, which led to frustration and depression. In CPA I began to learn that it was OK, even positive, to take care of myself and not push beyond my limits. I was encouraged to treat myself as a valued friend.

Soon I began to recognize the necessity of taking time to stop moving, stop doing, or even thinking. When I was resting I was accomplishing something very important—I was contributing to my well-being and improved health. Thinking of rest as accomplishing something instead of doing nothing helped me accept it as a desired way to spend time instead of thinking of it as a waste of time.

Setting aside time to restore my body and mind is now part of my daily schedule. I plan for one or more periods of respite every day and the result is that I feel less pain and more energy. Not only that, but recognizing the importance of rest gives me a life with more serenity.

Be content to progress in slow steps until you have legs to run and wings with which to fly.

PADRE PIO

Step Twelve: *"Having had a spiritual awakening as the result of these Steps, we tried to carry this message to others and to practice these principles in all our affairs."*

First, we have to work the first eleven Steps and have the spiritual awakening. I have found that even though I did this in other Twelve Step programs, when I arrived at CPA I had to start at Step One again and work my way through each Step. As I found in other programs, when I got to Step Twelve, I was a different person. The power of the program had changed me. And, as in other programs, I like to work the Steps again every couple of years. They are an effective tool, and I find they always improve my life.

Then, we carry the message to others. We can do this by sharing in meetings, doing service work, sponsoring others, and sharing our experience, strength, and hope.

And finally, in culmination of the whole process of the Twelve Steps, we strive to practice the principles in all our affairs. Something that came hard for me was to put myself first. But pain and illness have a way of teaching me to do this, whether I want to learn it or not.

So if all I can do today is pray for you as well as myself, then I am working the Twelfth Step and still honoring my own needs. Treating others kindly even though I feel miserable, am cranky, and want the whole world to go away—that is working my Twelfth Step. Telling a family member that I love them, and today I have nothing to give and am going to rest in my room for the day—that is practicing the principles of the program in all my affairs. Telling my friend I want to continue our friendship, but it will have to be by telephone because I don't have the energy to leave the house these days—that is working the Twelfth Step.

The Steps are in order because they build on each other. It is important to start with Step One and work through to Step Twelve. There is no single right way to work each Step. Whatever way works, however long it takes, is the right way, for every one of us.

Spiritual friendship, association with wise and noble friends, and wise and noble deeds are the whole of the holy life.

BUDDHA

When I first came into CPA I would get sick for a few days, then feel better for a few days. I started keeping track of the sick days vs. healthy days and calculated that I was sick about 60% of the time.

Most recently that has changed to 100% of the time, for about 7 months now. This has brought me to a new level of understanding of my illness, and I am now more convinced than ever that this illness is something to learn to cope with, not something that I will be able to get rid of.

A few years ago, I started looking at what had lifted my obsession in my first Twelve Step program. I now believe that it was a combination of the unity of the group (meetings and fellowship), Step work, and service. My goal in CPA is to use these three sides of the program, on a daily basis, on my chronic pain and chronic illness. With the phone meetings available, it isn't that hard to do.

I do my prayer and meditation in the morning, get to some kind of spiritual meeting (phone, face-to-face, Twelve Step, or church), do some Tenth Step writing at night, and do some act of service each day.

After a number of years of practicing, I now see that I feel a real sense of value, meaning, and purpose about my life, even when I can't accomplish many of the material or social goals I thought I "should" accomplish in my pre-CPA days. I get a sense that my life is valuable to others, and to me, just by working a good program each day and sharing my experience, strength, and hope with others. Many of my acts of service are as simple as making a call or writing a letter to a friend. The size of the act isn't important.

For me, it is comforting to know that all I have to do is work a good program and that will lead to making a real difference in the world.

If you want to be happy, be.

LEO TOLSTOY

My initial impression of meditation was of someone sitting cross-legged in a quiet room, repeating some inaudible mantra under their breath. I wasn't even sure exactly what meditation was meant to accomplish. I supposed it was for relaxation. It never crossed my mind that it could be about "*improving my conscious contact with God.*"

Then I became involved in Twelve Step recovery, and my mind began to open. I developed different ideas of what meditation was all about. I learned there were many different ways to meditate.

I learned to use meditation to help me relax, which has become a tool for living with pain. Sometimes I meditate just to try and connect with my higher self, and to quiet my busy mind. But most of my time can't be spent sitting in silent meditation. Like most of us, I must go about the business of living, even when I am in pain.

So now I practice constant meditation—the idea of "being in the moment with nonjudgmental awareness." It's something I can practice every moment of every day. When I'm not thinking about something that happened yesterday, or busy with thoughts of tomorrow, I am free to focus on right now. One day at a time, I practice staying mindful of my breath, my body, my thoughts, and my environment. When I do this, I have peace.

Faith is the opening of all sides and every level of one's life to the Divine inflow.

MARTIN LUTHER KING, JR.

It never occurred to me to pray for *"knowledge of His will for me and the power to carry that out."* My prayers were usually to ask God to get me out of some trouble I had gotten myself into, and usually some form of bargaining was involved as well. If my prayers weren't directly for me, they were for someone I loved or cared about.

As a result of working the Steps, I learned how to pray for unselfish things. Today my prayers may still include some requests for help, such as help with the pain, and help with the power to carry out God's will for me. I pray for patience, and I pray for the ability to see the lessons the pain brings to my life. And, I pray for the ability to hear and accept God's messages.

I am conscious of the words that come through my loved ones, my friends, and even perfect strangers. Messages come through the voice of my sponsor and others in recovery, through the music I listen to, and the books that I read. And, the messages don't always come in the form of words. They can be delivered in a loving hug from a child, or a smile from a stranger at just the right time. They can come in a dream or a series of coincidences. I've learned to pay attention when the same message seems to come from different sources. When I'm attentive to the moment, the messages are constant, clear, and undeniable.

Remember not only to say the right thing in the right place, but far more difficult still, to leave unsaid the wrong thing at the tempting moment.

BENJAMIN FRANKLIN

Recently I traveled to be at the bedside of my daughter, who was very ill with complications from surgery. I thought I'd be gone from home a week at the most, and would just visit her a few hours a day. Instead, there were twelve-hour shifts, day and night, sleeping on a chair in her room, and caring for my granddaughter when I wasn't needed at the hospital. Had I known ahead of time that this is what I'd be doing, I would have been terrified, sure that I couldn't possibly exert myself so much.

To my surprise, I was able to keep putting one foot in front of the other, continuing to help for three weeks. At that point I ran out of energy and realized that I'd be in the bed with my daughter if I didn't leave. By then her condition had improved enough that I felt she was no longer in danger.

I knew, without a doubt, that I was powerless not only over my own pain, but also the pain being suffered by my daughter. And I was powerless to make her better. I realized that my natural inclination to "take charge" wasn't going to work for my son-in-law, who is an organizer, planner, and controller, just as I am. So I turned my will and life over to God, suited up and showed up every morning, and asked my son-in-law what he needed each day.

Most important, the Eleventh Step became very clear to me. I had prayed for knowledge of God's will, and believed that I was where He wanted me. Most of the time, I was able to pray *only* for that, asking that all of us be given the strength we needed each moment. And I believed just as strongly that I only had to ask for the *"power to carry that out,"* and it was given to me. My program "worked me" the entire time.

What is real prayer? Praise to God. And the meaning of praise? Appreciating; thus opening the heart more and more to the divine beauty one sees in manifestation.

PIR-O-MURSHID HAZRAT INAYAT KHAN

My sponsor works the Steps by taking out the dictionary. He sits down at a table and goes through each Step, word by word, to truly understand its meaning. When I began Step Eleven I often would compare myself to others in the fellowship, thinking they were wise and spiritual, and I felt that I would never get there. I finally got up the nerve to ask my sponsor about it.

He asked where I thought I was having a problem. After much discussion he started to laugh. In his point of view the most important word in the whole Step, I had whizzed right by. The word that I missed was "improve." Nowhere in this Step does it state that we need to do it perfectly.

Since that day, I have taken my sponsor's advice to heart. I no longer see Step Eleven as referring to other people. This is a personal Step for me. This is where I can spend some time, each day, in communication with my Higher Power. I can thank him for all the gifts I receive: a smile from a stranger, a parking space, a door held open so I can get through on my wheelchair, a hug from my wife and son, a funny joke from a friend. I can ask for guidance in my life to understand the meaning of what I witness in this world.

I have a friend who says he doesn't necessarily pray to his Higher Power so much as he has a constant conversation as the day goes by. From this conversation he is able to move through the day without the fears he held for so many years.

So I pledge to myself today to continue to improve my conscious contact with God as I understand Him, praying only for knowledge of His will for me, and the power to carry that out.

I draw prayer round me like a dark protective wall, withdraw inside as one might into a convent cell and then step outside again, calmer and stronger and more collected.

Etty Hillesum

Daily prayer and meditation are a very important way to stay connected with my Higher Power. Over the years of growing in my CPA program, I have developed a relationship with a Higher Power that is just right for me. My routine includes prayer and meditation every morning.

This morning, however, I woke up and found myself hurrying around the house trying to get ready for my Twelve Step meeting—and I forgot prayer—Step Eleven. In the midst of my busyness I was replaying a resentment left over from yesterday. I jumped into my truck and went to pick up a sponsee. When he got into the truck he said, "You seem a little tense this morning." I started to complain about the events of yesterday and project the "what ifs" into tomorrow. I was very irritable and unreasonable.

While I was ranting I pulled down the overhead visor and a plastic card fell into my lap. It was a picture of someone kneeling in prayer. I recognized in that moment that I had been so caught up in my feelings of anger I'd forgotten to practice Step Eleven. When we arrived, my sponsee got out to join the meeting. I stayed in the truck and took time right then to be with my Higher Power in prayer and meditation. I became quiet and noticed yesterday and tomorrow drift away from my thinking. Because I did this, afterward I was able to walk into the meeting feeling serene.

To my surprise, the topic of the meeting was Prayer and Meditation! I laughed, knowing my Higher Power is always close by.

When we are willing to accept the dark emotions rather than conquer them, we become warriors of vulnerability, and we learn the way of surrender.

MIRIAM GREENSPAN

Step Eleven is sometimes called a maintenance Step. It allows us to keep our program going every day. In Steps One, Two, and Three we discovered that we had a Power greater than ourselves, and we turned our life and our will over. In this Step, we get to build on that relationship and our surrender to God's will.

Before CPA, I just called on my Higher Power when I was in trouble. Otherwise, I ignored him. I learned in CPA, that is no way to forge a relationship. I found that I need to stay in touch with my Higher Power all day, throughout the day, even on the good days. I discovered that as I maintained conscious contact, my trust and faith in my Higher Power grew.

"Thank you for this delicious peach. Thank you for this caring friend. Thank you for the birds singing outside my window." I can stay connected to my Higher Power when things are going well. "I'm scared. I'm worried. My friend is in trouble. Please help." I can stay in touch with my Higher Power when things are not going well.

My sponsor taught me to interpret Step Eleven as prayer when I speak to God, and meditation when I listen. I engage in many different forms of prayer and meditation. Walking through the woods, I can commune with God through nature while I talk and listen. Going to a religious center, I can pray and ask for guidance. Meditation can be done walking, or chanting, or being mindful of my breathing, even as I sit in a doctor's examination room.

One explanation of meditation is non-attached mindfulness, just being aware of the thoughts, emotions, and sensations passing through. Sometimes when the pain is present, I practice meditation by being aware of the sensations in my body, with no attachment to making them be different. Along with this, I can watch all the thoughts that show up, and hear them, but not have to react to them. Then I can hand it all over to my Higher Power, praying to know His will for me.

Step Eleven keeps my connection to my Higher Power strong. And my faith deepens.

Take rest; a field that has rested gives a bountiful crop.

OVID

Recently I was in the midst of one of my more productive days—scratching off item after item from my to-do list. Items that had been sitting there for many days, being ignored for no other reason than I would rather do it tomorrow or when I feel better...even these were getting done. I was on a roll, and planning on working through to the time for making dinner. Then I remembered how important it is to have quiet time just for myself. So late in the afternoon I got into my recliner and simply sat, quietly resting.

I take time on a daily basis to rest, and when my pain is abnormally high, I often meditate. This day, I felt great and was productive, and normally I would have pushed through right into the evening, but instead I took inventory of myself. During quiet times I am best able to feel what my body needs, and what my being needs. More rest? How are my basic bodily functions operating? What is my pain level and what, if anything, might have contributed to an increase or decrease in pain? How are my relationships with family? Any amends to make? What type of music do I want to listen to? What do I want to fix for dinner?

All of these things go through my mind when I relax and look at life on any particular day. I find that taking the time to relax and just concentrate on myself and my life, is vital to continued recovery from chronic pain and chronic illness.

One of the greatest discoveries a man makes, one of his greatest surprises, is to find he can do what he was afraid he couldn't do.

HENRY FORD

Step Eleven guides me, through prayer and meditation, to conscious contact with my Higher Power, my source of compassion. When I'm in physical pain, frustrated by it, spinning in the emotional pain I'm creating around it, I'm far from compassion. It is only with compassion for myself that I can begin to ease up and see that I'm *creating* the emotional pain. The physical discomfort simply exists. With the relief compassion provides, I can recognize that life is not as awful as it appears from my distorted perspective and I can actually experience a nice day.

And then, I find myself moving a little beyond feeling mired in the pain. Sometimes prayer and meditation leads me to my sponsor or another CPA friend, and their compassion touches mine. With their help, I transcend the inner struggles and shift my attitude, which gets me back into action.

It can be hard for me to encourage myself to meditate, so over the years I've had to discover various methods, places, and rituals to work this part of the Eleventh Step. When I sit down to meditate I often find it helpful to begin with a guided meditation, guided imagery, or a chant. After I've meditated, I often write. My life in every sense is better when I do work this Step. God's will for me usually becomes clear, most times not at that moment, but later.

Then I may have to wind my way back through this Step to find the energy to *"carry that out."* I'm learning new paths and approaches to pray and meditate all the time.

JOY

The most completely wasted of all days is that in which we have not laughed.

Nicolas Chamfort

I love reading and practicing the *One Day at a Time* sayings from our literature. My favorite this week is: "*One Day at a Time* I will enjoy something that is fun." I find laughing is the most fun thing I can do. I once was told that when we laugh it releases endorphins that actually make us feel better. Laughter causes me to forget about pain, at least temporarily. Laughter may not cure chronic pain or chronic illness, but it does help me to recover from its disabling effects.

Laughter also helps me to not take myself too seriously. There have been times I have done something embarrassing, and when I look back on it I can laugh at myself. Some of these things were hurtful, and yet I can still find the ability to laugh. Sometimes I have a choice between laughing and crying. My motto is, "If I have already cried about it and am still disturbed, then why not give laughing a try?"

Laughter can relieve emotional stress, and I find that emotional stress is a major contributor to my chronic pain levels. I've been told that laughing boosts my immune system. Laughter may, in fact, be the best medicine.

Today I will allow myself a few chuckles and chortles—alone, or with others. I will continue to make this part of my program. I will read or watch something funny. I will remember to laugh at myself too, and not take life too seriously.

When we are no longer able to change a situation, we are challenged to change ourselves.

Victor Frankl

In the past, I believed that being physically ill precluded being happy. It was an axiom that ruled out any chance of being happy again in my life. Being told that I had a choice as to how happy I was going to be was a revelation, and one I did not believe possible at first. I thought of myself as a victim, stuck with my rotten lot in life. But I wanted to believe that although I might not ever get well, I could get happy.

Over the years in the program I have learned that what I give my attention to is what grows, just as in a garden. If I water the weeds, they will grow. If I water the flowers, they will grow. It is up to me to decide what I want in my garden. I can be happy if I want to be. Of course, I have to be willing to let go of my misery, to release my victim thinking, and to consider new possibilities. Sometimes it is letting go of the old ways that is the hardest step for me to take.

The pain and illness are going to be present no matter what my attitude. However, whether my life is filled with happiness or misery is my choice. Which would I prefer? Put like that, of course I want to be happy. Since this is my life, I would rather it be one I enjoy. It is up to me to learn how to water the flowers and let those weedy attitudes dry up and fall away.

Don't be concerned about being disloyal to your pain by being joyous.

Pir Vilayat Inayat Khan

At my first CPA meeting I heard people laughing and describing fun events in their lives. I assumed their pain and illness were not nearly as bad as mine. But as I listened, I heard that others had gone through trials equally as difficult as mine and had found a way to smile again. They were currently in pain, yet managed to enjoy life. I did not understand how this was possible, but I wanted to believe that there was hope, so I kept coming back.

There were long periods of time, when I was first ill, that joy was completely obliterated from my life. I lost my spouse, my career, and my house. There seemed to be nothing to feel happy about. I went from one loss to another, and resigned myself to a life of misery.

Sometimes I get so lost in the pain and illness that I forget I can also surrender to the joy. I find myself caught in all-or-nothing thinking. All pain with no room for joy. I've learned they can co-exist, even in the same moment.

While facing pain, there is often joy to be discovered in small wonders—the ease of breathing, quiet moments of peaceful rest, simple kindnesses from friends, an intimate connection to my Higher Power. It is so good to be reminded that it is okay, in fact way more than okay, to find the joy, the silver linings, and the unexpected peace that come in the midst of life's challenges.

We have within us a limitless supply of new beginnings.
JOAN FITZGERALD

I might be able to be happy even if I don't feel like it. One day last week I was feeling particularly unhappy. I was depressed, and it seemed that the hours were stretching drearily ahead of me. I endured those hours until they faded and I was my "regular" self again.

Then it hit me. I could have done something about my unhappiness and lessened it sooner. I know from past experience that by choice I can often improve my sense of well-being. It takes a decision, and it takes effort, but I have resources and tools. It helps me to have some things written down. If I can drag myself to some of my literature or slogans or lists, it gives me a jump-start in a positive direction. I don't have to think up helpful things when I don't feel like it, I just have to get myself to go look over some literature that is already available!

If I feel down or sad or miserable, that is OK. It's perfectly acceptable for me to have these feelings, but after a while it's time to turn and focus my mind elsewhere. There are good things in life, and if I spend some time remembering them, my happiness will increase. I have to make up my mind to do this, which isn't an easy thing to do when I'm blue, but it is often effective. Little things like being thankful for a grandchild, or a breeze, or a good book, or a memory of a good time, can ease me back toward happiness. I can start my day over, anytime I want.

Plenty of people miss their share of happiness, not because they never found it, but because they didn't stop to enjoy it.

WILLIAM FEATHER

When I look closely at a situation, my perspective is limited. When I step back and widen the horizon, however, I see a larger panorama of life. I notice the sky is blue, the flowers are beautiful, birds are singing. I stop getting caught up in myself, and all the things I think I need to be happy.

Before getting ill, I lived in the fast lane, going 75 miles per hour. Rushing from Point A to Point B, I didn't see a thing in between. Now I am in the slow lane, going 40 miles per hour, and on a daily basis I see friendship, love, and the gifts that my Higher Power presents to me.

Today my life is a mystery. I don't understand it completely, but I don't have to. It is a gift from my Higher Power. He has given me the opportunity to participate in life, which I think of as a joyous adventure, even with my physical limitations. My cancer and arthritis have no bearing on my outlook on life, because my thinking is positive, and I bring my Higher Power with me 24 hours a day.

When I get up in the morning I thank God for this day, and at night I continue to thank Him.

A man cannot directly choose his circumstances, but he can choose his thoughts, and so indirectly, yet surely, shape his circumstances.

JAMES ALLEN

Happiness is an inside job. If happiness came from something outside of myself, I'd be miserable all the time. Well, that is exactly how I was before finding CPA. I was miserable: because on the day of a party my illness was out of control and I had to stay home; because my children were going trick-or-treating and I couldn't go with them; because my husband could no longer live with my illness and asked for a divorce; because best friends disappeared when I could no longer keep up. The list goes on and on.

It wasn't until I completely surrendered my beliefs about how I thought life should be and opened my mind to new possibilities that I could begin to find happiness. It took a change in my thinking, so that I could see the opportunities for growth and find love, acceptance, and serenity.

I had to ask myself if I wanted to continue being so unhappy and miserable. Since I could not find a cure or treatment, I had to focus on the solution, not the problem. And the solution was in me, not outside of me.

Since this is a spiritual program of recovery, it was not totally my doing. I had to work the Steps and turn myself over to the care of my Higher Power. It was my Higher Power who lifted the dark lenses from my eyes and helped me to see what was good in my life. It was my friends in the fellowship who reminded me that my illness did not take away my basic humanity—my ability to love, to have compassion, to be kind. My illness had removed me from the mainstream of life, and now, freed from chasing cures, I was given the gift of time. I could meditate and pray and begin to experience peace and serenity.

In CPA I have received new tools that guide me towards happiness. Instead of despairing and being filled with rage, I can choose to respond to the challenges of my illness with an open mind, creating space for my Higher Power to work in my life in unexpected ways. Is this always easy? Emphatically, no. The key is to keep coming back and practicing in small ways every day.

HOPE

The grateful heart sits at a continuous feast.

Proverbs 15:15

Pain is subjective. We can't compare pains any more than we can compare beauty. Each one of us is unique. I can never know what your pain feels like. But this is not important. Nor does it matter whether we abhor taking medications, whether we are addicts, or whether we are happy about taking medications. The point is that we have the CPA program to help us live in peace and serenity with all aspects of our pain and illness.

We learn in CPA that we have choices. We have a Higher Power, and that is where our strength and our guidance come from, about medications and all issues. No one has the final say, not doctors or the family or the fellowship. We get to have choices about our attitude and about how we take care of ourselves, which includes our medications.

We learn to pray for the knowledge of God's will and the power to carry it out. And if we are guided to take medications, then we can trust that today this is the next indicated action. We get to use the tool of "One Day at a Time." We don't know what will come next. We do know that for this day, we are cared for by our Higher Power and He will guide us.

We get to make amends to ourselves for any past misuse of drugs. We get to use them responsibly today. Whatever we did in the past is no longer relevant. We are powerless over the past, over our pain and illness. In CPA we have the tool of accepting "what is," for this day only. It is the way we can move forward in serenity. My prayer is, "God, help me to have the best day possible with any circumstances."

We also have the tool of gratitude: for the miracles of modern medicine, for the comfort of safe homes, for the friends and family who support us, for the government helping us out. The list can go on.

The gift of CPA is that in unity and recovery, loved and guided by our Higher Power, we find our way out of suffering and into happiness and celebration of life. This is a program of hope.

For the grateful person knows that God is good, not by hearsay but by experience. And that is what makes all the difference.

THOMAS MERTON

I had more than fifty years of relatively good health, so I'm having a difficult time learning to accept the reality of the limitations of my illness. Today I am paying the price for overdoing it. I made a decision on Saturday to help someone move, by packing some boxes for them. I knew the consequences could be days of increased pain but chose to do it anyway. I am feeling very low today, depressed, and tired of hurting.

After being immersed in these feelings for a while, I decided to look at some of the Twelve Step tools I have been given over the past few months, and try to get out of this negative state.

I need to trust that whatever happens, wherever I am, I am in the right spot in God's plan.

I can accept what is and turn it over to God, even if I have to do this continuously.

I can try to turn it over to my Higher Power, and if I don't like it I can take it back. When I am ready, I can turn it over again.

I can allow life to unfold on God's terms. This means that I cannot always do what I want or think I should do. I need to be willing to accept God's will and to accept what my reality is now.

These are all ideas that have been given to me, in one form or another, by others, and are by no means ideas that I have as part of me. They are things that I am in the process of learning. I love the slogan, "Progress, Not Perfection." It is so comforting. I don't have to do it all now.

The cool thing is, I am just beginning to delve into this program and there is so much more to see and learn and experience. That gives me hope for a more serene future.

I think a hero is an ordinary individual who finds the strength to persevere and endure in spite of overwhelming obstacles. They are the real heroes, and so are the families and friends who have stood by them.

CHRISTOPHER REEVE

Being active is a vital help for my chronic pain. I am a paraplegic. I used to think that due to my condition, age, and chronic pain I would just be stuck in my wheelchair, put on weight, and live out my life quietly.

That was then. Now I live an active and fulfilling life, because I do exercise, I do laps around a soccer field by my house in the chair, and have physical therapy two days a week. I have started a weight-loss program as well, losing 16 pounds so far. I was able to do this because of CPA. I am probably in the best physical shape I ever have been in.

This program is based on the Twelve Steps for a reason. It works. And that's because it is centered on recovery. Getting started is hard work. It takes a willingness to break through old belief systems. There were times in my first Twelve Step work that I felt old-timers were jumping on me, but I listened, did what they suggested, kept coming back, and recovered "One Day at a Time."

Why I keep coming back to CPA is because of my group's willingness to listen to and understand me without my needing to explain myself. That can only be found in CPA. Here, I can share my life's experience, all the ups and downs of living as they pertain to chronic pain or chronic illness. Why I am in chronic pain or chronic illness makes no difference. What makes a difference is that I am not sitting idly, watching the world go by. I am the one going by!

To the newcomers, please be patient with yourselves and be patient with us old-timers. As an old-timer, I will try to be patient with you, through thick and thin, unreservedly, as long as it takes for the miracle of changed attitudes to result in a changed life.

Paradoxically, we achieve true wholeness only by embracing our fragility and sometimes, our brokenness. Wholeness is a natural radiance of Love, and Love demands that we allow the destruction of our old self for the sake of the new.

JALAJA BONHEIM

Chronic pain is relatively new to me, so I am in the process of grieving. Realizing that the pain is indeed chronic and may be with me for the rest of my life can be daunting, after over fifty years of taking good health for granted. This is something I never expected in life, and I was totally unprepared.

Acceptance seems to be key. I remember reading about the three phases of grieving. In denial, I see myself trying to keep up with my past responsibilities and expectations, from both myself and others. When I do this, I end up feeling worse physically. But it is not easy to give up my old self-image. As time goes on I find it easier to let go, but often relapse into this old thinking. I have to remind myself: "Progress, Not Perfection."

In the extreme emotional pain phase, I sometimes experience despair, depression, overwhelming sadness, and guilt. Sometimes I just hurt and cry, sometimes I go to my CPA and Twelve Step resources and read, sometimes I talk with someone who understands, or make a gratitude list. It is not easy to do these things, but if I make the effort it often helps.

When I can be in acceptance, the relief is great. I accept the new circumstances in my life, and the pressure is lifted. If I can be in my "new" reality, then I can deal with what is, instead of continuously trying to swim upstream. I am learning to make better choices for myself, trying to learn to trust in my Higher Power and believe that this new life must somehow be part of the perfect plan for me.

It is true that having chronic illness and pain is giving me opportunities for growth. There is a richness of life that I sometimes have now that was missing before, much of it because I am developing the strength necessary to live this type of life, and much of it because of the fellowship of CPA. I have hope for a better life in spite of unpleasant circumstances, and am experiencing many new things. Sounds crazy when I think about it, but it's true.

If you assume there's no hope, you guarantee there will be no hope.

NOAM CHOMSKY

Hope can be so elusive when we are in pain, have lost our independence, and have lost our life as we knew it. Arousing hope is desirable, but how do we find it under the stresses that occur from living with chronic pain and illness?

My experience of evoking hope when I am hopeless is still new and tentative, but I have been able to find hope a couple of times by practicing some things I have recently learned. Sometimes I have to exercise my will to take the steps toward hope. I jot down meaningful statements and slogans when I hear them. This list of inner resources is one of the first places I will go when I feel despair, but sometimes I have to urge myself to read it.

Another thing I do is to look over the CPA literature. It takes effort to begin this process, but reading positive words will slowly open the door to the renewal of hope. I have found that taking this one action can snowball into feeling peaceful and optimistic again. I am very thankful that God has provided these tools for me.

When I am feeling low, it seems that I am not motivated to call my sponsor or others who are available to help. But as time goes on, I am seeing that if I do reach out, I will hear something that eases my suffering in some way. It's amazing to see how God uses the members in the program to bring each other comfort and encouragement. We are placed in each other's lives for a reason.

Feeling hopeless can be so devastating, and seems to be understandable for us, but little by little I think I can learn to experience hope more often. It might take practice, but it's worth giving it a try.

Character consists of what you do on the third and fourth tries.

JAMES MICHENER

Someone asked me recently what I "do." Meaning, of course, what kind of work do I engage in. It got me thinking about the long journey I have been on since the day I became ill.

It was all very difficult and frightening at first. There was so much loss in going from a healthy, active young woman to being bedbound and feeling like I was ninety years old. Once we are knocked down flat for a long period of time we are cautious when we become more active again. Our bodies can become de-conditioned, whether our movement is limited due to surgery or an accident or chronic illness. I remember the first time I went to a grocery store after being home for many months. Along with the lack of energy overall, I was overwhelmed with the stimulation overload and felt dizzy. I had to move back into the world very slowly.

For many years I was afraid to try anything new. It seemed like the controlled world I lived in worked well, and if I dared risk going beyond it I'd put myself into a relapse or increase the pain. There was no Twelve Step program in my life back then, but there was a Higher Power who cared about me and guided me gently back into the world.

When some energy and motivation returned, at first I had a tendency to do too much. In CPA, however, I learned about doing half what I had planned. This taught me how to practice "Easy Does It." I learned how to be patient and "Keep it Simple." There was a lot of returning to square one again and again. It was three steps forward and two steps back...or, harder yet, four steps back. With baby steps I discovered that I could live a quality life, filled with the things I love doing, when I take it slowly. I thought I'd never travel again, yet years later I took a trip abroad.

All that said, I have good years, months, and days. And bad ones. I have learned that if I am down, I may not be down forever, and if I am up, I may not be up forever. The pain may be unbearable one day, and manageable the next. As I let go of trying to control how my day looks, and turn it all over to my Higher Power, I am able to be content with whatever shows up.

APPENDICES

Printed by permission of Alcoholics Anonymous

THE TWELVE STEPS OF CHRONIC PAIN ANONYMOUS

1. We admitted we were powerless over pain and illness—that our lives had become unmanageable.

2. Came to believe that a Power greater than ourselves could restore us to sanity.

3. Made a decision to turn our will and our lives over to the care of God, *as we understood Him.*

4. Made a searching and fearless moral inventory of ourselves.

5. Admitted to God, to ourselves, and to another human being the exact nature of our wrongs.

6. Were entirely ready to have God remove all these defects of character.

7. Humbly asked Him to remove our shortcomings.

8. Made a list of all persons we had harmed and became willing to make amends to them all.

9. Made direct amends to such people wherever possible, except when to do so would injure them or others.

10. Continued to take personal inventory and when we were wrong, promptly admitted it.

11. Sought through prayer and meditation to improve our conscious contact with God *as we understood Him*, praying only for knowledge of His will for us and the power to carry that out.

12. Having had a spiritual awakening as the result of these steps, we tried to carry this message to others with chronic pain and chronic illness, and to practice these principles in all our affairs.

Printed by Permission of Alcoholics Anonymous

THE TWELVE TRADITIONS OF CHRONIC PAIN ANONYMOUS

1. Our common welfare should come first, personal recovery depends upon CPA unity.

2. For our group purpose there is but one ultimate authority—a loving God as He may express Himself in our group conscience. Our leaders are but trusted servants; they do not govern.

3. The only requirement for CPA membership is a desire to recover from the emotional and spiritual debilitation of chronic pain or chronic illness.

4. Each group should be autonomous except in matters affecting other groups or CPA as a whole.

5. Each group has but one primary purpose—to carry its message to people living with chronic pain and chronic illness.

6. A CPA group ought never endorse, finance, or lend the CPA name to any outside enterprise, lest problems of money, property, and prestige divert us from our primary purpose.

7. Every CPA group ought to be fully self-supporting, declining outside contributions.

8. Chronic Pain Anonymous should remain forever non-professional, but our service centers may employ special workers.

9. CPA, as such, ought never be organized, but we may create service boards or committees directly responsible to those they serve.

10. Chronic Pain Anonymous has no opinion on outside issues; hence the CPA name ought never be drawn into public controversy.

11. Our public relations policy is based on attraction rather than promotion, we need always maintain personal anonymity at the level of press, radio, television, film, and the Internet.

12. Anonymity is the spiritual foundation of all our traditions, ever reminding us to place principles before personalities.

ONE DAY AT A TIME

One Day At A Time – I will make an effort to participate in the world. I will reach out and connect with another person. I can pick up the phone and call a friend, greet someone on the street, or I can smile at the clerk in the store.

One Day At A Time – I will put my focus on promoting the well-being of someone besides myself. I will take the attention off of me and my issues, and place it on the needs of another being.

One Day At A Time – I will pace myself and trust my body to guide me. I will not push when my body tells me it's time to stop. I will do half of what I think I can accomplish.

One Day At A Time – I will eat well and exercise in moderation. I will take an interest in my appearance and tend to my personal hygiene. I may dress comfortably, but I will try to look my very best.

One Day At A Time – I will ask for help when I need it. I will accept assistance graciously and be thankful. I will appreciate the people in my life who support me.

One Day At A Time – I will live each day to the best of my ability and take responsibility for my own happiness. I will notice the good in life and not dwell on the negative. I will count my blessings and enjoy all that I've been given.

One Day At A Time – I will remember that I am more than my pain or my illness. I will believe that I am perfect exactly as I am. I will accept whatever comes my way with an attitude of gratitude.

One Day At A Time – I will make an extra effort to be patient and gentle with myself and others when I am feeling irritable and frustrated. No blame, no shame. Just because I am in pain, doesn't mean I have to be a pain.

One Day At A Time – I will create some quiet moments for myself. I can use them for inner reflection, reviewing my day, or strengthening my spiritual connections. Taking this time each day is a rich and rewarding gift to myself.

One Day At A Time – I will enjoy something that is fun. I will engage my mind in creative activities. I will try something different and be open to new possibilities.

One Day At A Time – I accept the conditions of my life as they are this day. Within any condition I can contribute to myself, my family, and my community. I am a valuable member of society.

One Day At A Time – I will acknowledge feelings of fear and anxiety as they rise up. When they appear, I will remember to put my trust in a Power greater than myself. I will have hope in knowing that this, too, shall pass, and I will have faith that I can thrive through anything when I do it one moment at a time.

INDEX

A

acceptance xiii, xiv, 10, 11, 19-31, 55, 108, 118, 128
    of help, 102
    of medication, 2, 53
    of pain/powerlessness, 3, 8, 34, 53, 56, 114
    of responsibility, 74, 105
    of what is, 9, 26, 39, 47, 57, 59, 63, 76, 78, 84, 86, 91, 110, 115, 136, 137, 138, 140
    self, 4, 71, 79, 80, 83, 89, 93, 101, 134
acting "as if" 6, 28, 68, 107
addiction 2, 53, 60, 62, 137
aging 32, 45
alcoholic 2, 30, 57
Alcoholics Anonymous xi, 16, 65
amends 67, 129
    to ourselves, 72, 73, 74, 107, 137
anger 12-18, 66, 67, 90, 96, 99, 119
    holding on to, 7, 10
    toward God, 8, 24, 73
    over illness/pain, xiv, 8, 11, 30, 43, 57, 65, 104, 113, 115
    managing, 68, 69, 70, 72, 97, 118, 127
anonymity 103
anxiety 13, 25, 49, 104, 115
appearance/grooming 6, 64, 8
attitude 55, 86-98, 132
    changing, xiv, 18, 64, 71, 75, 78, 82, 102, 107, 111, 130, 139

attitude *continued*
    choosing, 132, 135, 137
    positive, 16, 28, 112, 115

B

belief systems 34, 35, 87, 91, 136, 139
blame 7, 18, 65, 68, 71
    God, 2, 27, 118
    self, 4, 34, 70
body 7, 19, 20, 21, 25, 32, 46, 48, 53, 61, 64, 69, 77, 90, 96, 102, 123, 128, 142
    angry with, 8, 72, 96
    care of, 118, 120, 129
    focus on, 57, 80
    spirit healed despite, xiv, 28, 38, 57, 79, 95
    wanting to change, 18, 24, 86, 101
bondage of self 103

C

cane 21, 94, 103
character defects 7, 66, 76, 83, 96
    triggered by feeling poorly, 72
    turning over to Higher Power, 24, 42, 97, 114
    See also shortcomings
choices 15, 44, 62,
    accepting consequences for, 110, 114
    gratitude for, 21, 91
    in how to live/behave, 4, 6, 30, 75, 76, 88, 96, 109, 116, 119, 132, 134, 137, 140

choices *continued*
to laugh, 131
compassion xiii, 10, 30, 72, 77, 89,
112, 130, 136
for self/body, xiv, 21, 61, 87
instead of envy, 97, 109
of friends, 99
courage 13, 21, 24, 44, 60-64, 71,
85, 97, 104, 113
See also Serenity Prayer
CPA fellowship, *See* fellowship/
friends, in CPA

D

denial 11, 19, 26, 84, 118, 140
depression 16, 30, 65, 78, 90, 94,
104, 120
and grief, 11, 20, 140
on bad days, 85, 115, 134, 138
working with, 13, 76, 117
doctors xiii, 2, 20, 30, 34, 37, 45,
48, 57, 61, 62, 65, 69, 71, 113,
128, 137

E

exercise 53, 78, 139, 147

F

faith 8, 13, 38-49, 85, 102, 124,
128
and fear, 15, 20, 49
in Higher Power, xv, 7, 9, 10,
11, 22, 26, 27, 62, 113, 128
See also God, Higher Power
fear xiv, 11, 12-18, 20, 22, 46, 57,
61, 62, 76, 80, 104, 117, 118,
142
and faith, 49, 100, 126
for the future, xiii, 31, 58, 64,
72, 104

fear *continued*
of using medication, 53
fellowship/friends in CPA xi, 28,
32, 44, 48, 63, 77, 99-107, 111,
122, 126, 137, 140, 141
support of, xv, 4, 9, 10, 12, 14,
15, 16, 17, 18, 21, 24, 35,
36, 38, 67, 87, 85, 136, 139
First Three Steps 8, 15, 42, 44, 48,
55, 128
See also, Step One; Step Two;
Step Three
fun 63, 110, 131, 133

G

God 1, 2, 8, 14, 28, 33, 34, 40, 41,
45, 50, 58, 60, 77, 81, 87, 93,
101, 102, 123, 138
blaming, 8, 24, 27, 32, 72, 73,
118
kindness of, 106
guidance of, 28, 31, 37, 39, 55,
56, 57, 59, 62, 85, 91
prayers to, 19, 124, 125, 126,
128, 137
love of, 17, 44, 46, 47
removing shortcomings, 33,
42, 83, 96
thanking, 29, 94, 135
God's pile and my pile 114
"going to the hardware store to
buy a loaf of bread" 86
gratitude 38, 90, 138, 147
powerful tool, 10
for the pain, 104
for what we have, 20, 24, 27,
31, 47, 54, 91, 95, 128,
134, 137
lists, 89, 93, 115, 140

grief 8, 9, 10, 11, 31, 41, 58, 115, 140

guilt 1, 58, 63, 70, 78, 83, 119, 140

H

happiness 8, 25, 31, 32, 33, 38, 48, 49, 106, 137
   an inside job, 136
   from a shift in attitude, 68, 86, 91, 96, 123, 134, 135
   not incompatible with pain/ disease, xiv, 7, 20, 28, 98, 66, 117, 132, 133

health 32, 34, 80, 87, 90, 96, 109, 122
   care for, 118, 119, 120; *See also* self-care
   loss of, 7, 9, 27, 107, 138, 142
   problems, 61, 78, 89
   taking for granted, 140

Higher Power 7, 34, 36, 49, 79, 86, 87, 101, 106, 112, 113, 135, 140
   and anger, 14, 73
   drugs as, 2
   help of, 22, 33, 26, 45, 56, 57, 60, 62, 67, 69, 71, 74, 76, 100, 113, 115, 117, 136, 138, 142
   removing defects, 24, 42, 66, 83
   sanity restored by, 35, 46, 47, 48, 58, 97
   there for me/us, 8, 9, 11, 32, 38, 42, 61, 102
   through prayer & meditation, 40, 43, 52, 69, 71, 77, 117, 126, 127, 128, 130

Higher Power *continued*
   turning it over to, 4, 13, 15, 20, 26, 37, 39, 43, 50, 51, 54, 55, 77, 80, 102, 108, 109, 137
   See also God

holiday 74, 91

hope xiv, 15, 20, 25, 45, 62, 72, 84, 113, 137-144
   through the fellowship, 2, 38, 101, 102, 121, 122
   without, 2, 30, 39, 40, 47, 57, 94, 95, 118

humility 23, 28, 30, 33, 70, 89, 104, 114

I

inventory 17, 29, 70, 71, 72, 75, 129, 145

isolation xiv, 10, 16, 38, 65, 90, 94, 99, 104, 107, 108, 111

J

joy xi, xv, 10, 12, 18, 22, 37, 91, 118, 131-136
   lost/diminished, 14, 39, 57
   steps/tools lead to, 38, 44, 113
   through service, 105
   with pain/illness, 7, 20, 117

"Just because I am in pain, doesn't mean I have to be a pain" 75

L

laughter 22, 25, 99, 131, 133

literature, CPA, 15, 44, 47, 50, 77, 78, 79, 104, 115, 131, 134, 140, 141

loneliness 17, 62, 111

loss 9-11, 27, 38, 47, 48, 88, 94, 141, 142

    mourning, 7, 8, 20, 21, 31, 99

    lessons from, 89, 102

    of dreams, 41

    of family/friends, 7, 17, 99, 133, 136

    of spontaneity, 110

love 10, 21, 30, 34, 38, 48, 61, 70, 79, 82, 102, 112, 117, 124, 136, 140

    of friends/family, 91, 93, 99, 108, 119, 121

    of God, 7, 8, 9, 13, 17, 24, 26, 33, 34, 37, 46, 47, 57, 135, 137

    of life, xiii, 7, 35, 98, 142

    of the fellowship, 12, 21, 36, 101, 104

    not worthy of, 34, 87

    self/body, 4, 7, 21, 24, 78, 87, 96

    with partner, 71, 72, 110

M

medications 2, 13, 20, 30, 31, 40, 46, 48, 53, 61, 62, 94, 108, 110, 137

meditation 15, 61, 69, 82, 117, 118, 122, 123, 127, 129, 130

meetings xiii, xv, 9, 30, 41, 77, 90, 105, 122, 127

    anonymity in, 103

    attending, 35, 44, 47, 49, 50, 90, 107

    sharing at, 106, 121

    things heard at, 6, 15, 22, 24, 37, 66, 67, 71, 85, 100, 101, 102, 133

miracles 7, 26, 28, 39, 40, 56, 89, 104, 108, 139

O

obstacles 66; *See also* character defects; shortcomings

"One Day at a Time" bookmark 75, 115, 131

"one elbow technique" 82

P

pain 3, 1-8, 16, 17, 32, 38, 40, 41, 43, 59, 116, 122

    as an excuse, 75, 68, 88

    emotional, 23, 26, 62, 65, 67, 72, 94, 95, 115, 130, 140

    bad days, 6, 8, 25, 30, 32, 34, 61, 68, 71, 73, 74, 75, 79, 87, 96, 98, 106, 115, 122, 136, 138

    focused on, 5, 80, 109, 112

    growth from, 10, 88, 89, 104, 105

    increased intensity, 9, 11, 26, 31, 40, 45, 49, 65, 76, 85, 94, 95, 113, 114, 129, 142

    lessened by service, 106, 109, 111, 112

    not alone with, 12, 61, 16, 99, 102

    fighting, 21, 23, 55, 60, 78, 86

    taking it out on others, 67, 68, 70, 71, 75

paraplegic 81, 93, 139

physical intimacy 110

powerlessness 12, 32, 37, 41, 45, 48, 97, 104, 116, 125, 145

    accepting/admitting, 3, 4, 8, 15, 20, 23, 25, 26, 55, 56, 61, 108, 137

prayer 31, 33, 40, 45, 49, 50, 59, 69, 79, 93, 122-128, 130, 137
See also Serenity Prayer

R

relapse 22, 42, 59, 87, 115, 142
responsibility 30, 63, 74, 137
for tasks, 78, 105, 120, 140
for attitude/behavior, 33, 34, 65, 68, 71, 87
See also accountability
rest 22, 58, 59, 61, 74, 78, 79, 116, 119, 120, 121, 129, 133

S

sanity 35, 46, 47, 48, 58, 87, 97
self-care 19, 26, 74, 77, 78, 91, 109, 110, 116-130, 137
self-pity 8, 10, 16, 31, 48, 61, 65, 90, 101, 104, 107
Serenity Prayer vii, 14, 15, 18, 41, 46, 50, 93
serenity xiv, xv, 6
despite fear, 15
program/tools for, xi, 44, 47, 58, 71, 84, 120, 136, 137
through acceptance, 19, 24, 136, 137
with help of Higher Power, 12, 22, 32, 35, 38, 42, 76
See also Serenity Prayer
service xiii, 39, 97, 105, 106, 107, 109, 121, 122, 125
shortcomings 33, 83, 114; *See also* character defects
sleep 60, 96, 110
slogans 7, 13, 64, 82, 105, 134, 141, 142

slogans *continued*
"Don't compare your insides with another person's outside," 64
"Don't quit five minutes before the miracle," 7
"Easy Does It," 22, 61, 142
"FEAR – Face Everything And Recover," 13
"First Things First," 15
"Keep it Simple," 142
"Just For Today," 26, 42, 59, 68, 86, 95, 113, 115, 118
"Let Go and Let God," 43, 46, 55, 61, 91, 95, 102
"One Day at a Time," xv, 2, 10, 15, 24, 26, 75, 80, 92, 113, 115, 118, 123, 131, 137, 139
"Progress, Not Perfection," 80, 81, 110, 119, 138, 140
"Replace Fear with Faith," 13
"This, too, shall pass," 10, 32, 95, 115, 147
"Three A's: Awareness, Acceptance, and Action," 59
"We have to give it away to keep it," 105
"What you think of me is none of my business," 64, 80
sponsor 67, 101, 109, 116, 121, 124, 126, 127, 130
talking to, 15, 18, 50, 61, 71, 97, 104, 115, 141
working Steps with, 7, 26, 39, 47, 69, 73, 74, 83, 94, 100, 128

Step One 20, 23, 37, 56, 61, 70, 104, 121
  benefits of, 3, 25,
  seems counter-intuitive, 57
  working with sponsor on, 26, 28
  See also First Three Steps
Step Two 35, 46, 58, 102
  See also First Three Steps
Step Three 27, 37, 50, 51, 60
  See also First Three Steps
Step Four 14, 16, 17, 70, 72, 75, 76
Step Five 83
Step Six 42
Step Seven 33, 114
Step Eight 67, 73, 76
Step Nine 74
Step Ten 70, 71, 122
Step Eleven 61, 79, 123, 124, 125, 126, 127, 128, 130
Step Twelve 106, 121
strength xiv, 9, 12, 49, 71, 76, 79-85, 93, 102, 109, 125, 137, 139
  from the fellowship, xi, 16, 97, 104, 121, 122, 140
  of God, 2, 11, 35, 61, 119, 125
surrender 50-59, 84, 133
  and Higher Power, 7, 9, 20, 28, 35, 41, 128
  praying for, 8, 11, 38
  through acceptance, 7, 25, 86, 136

T
teachable xiv, 28, 56, 103
"Thy will, not mine, be done" vii, 18, 41, 50
  See also Serenity Prayer
Tools of the Program 82, 87, 123, 137
  about, xiii, 18, 38, 58, 61, 102, 107, 113, 115, 136
  use of, 10, 15, 28, 46, 51, 59, 78, 97, 106, 116, 121, 134, 138, 141
Tradition Four 77
trust 32-37, 100, 101, 137
  in Higher Power, xv, 9, 10, 22, 45, 50, 61, 62, 80, 97, 115, 128, 138, 140
Twelve Steps 39, 44, 47, 51, 61, 69, 72, 90, 94, 121, 145
Twelve Traditions of Chronic Pain Anonymous 146

W
weight gain/loss 94, 139
wheelchair 29-30, 63, 92, 93, 126, 139
working the program 39, 44, 65, 81, 83, 91, 93, 102, 121
writing 17, 95, 122, 130

LITERATURE AVAILABLE FROM CHRONIC PAIN ANONYMOUS

What is CPA? Brochure

Can CPA Help? Brochure

One Day at a Time, Explained Brochure

One Day at a Time Bookmark

CPA literature can be purchased or downloaded at:
www.chronicpainanonymous.org

The website lists the US and Canada telephone, online, and face-to-face groups for anyone seeking to attend a CPA meeting. You can also learn how to start a CPA group in your community.

To contact CPA directly, send an email to:
info@chronicpainanonymous.org

Or write to:
Chronic Pain Anonymous Service Board
8912 E. Pinnacle Peak Road
Suite F9-628
Scottsdale AZ 85255

NOTES

17856813R00091

Made in the USA
Charleston, SC
04 March 2013